IMAGES
of America
HOBBS AND LEA COUNTY

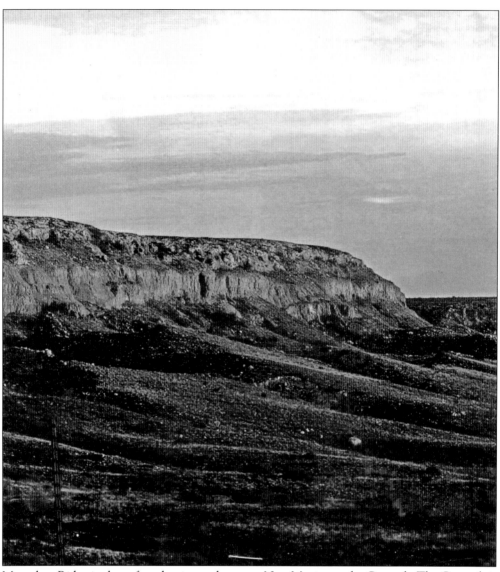

Mescalero Ridge is also referred to in southeastern New Mexico as the Caprock. The Caprock is about 28 miles from Tatum, New Mexico. Between the 1500s and the 1600s, New Mexico was ruled by Spain from the capital in Mexico City; many exploratory missions were sent north to Santa Fe. These expeditions drew maps and kept meticulous records, and they named points of interest and landmarks, and usually traveled close to the Pecos River or Rio Grande for water. One group followed the eastern side of the Pecos and discovered the Mescalero Ridge, or the Caprock. The officer drawing the map named it the Estacada because it resembled an escarpment or palisade. Scouts climbed the ridge and were amazed at the cast level plain that reached out east as far as they could see, and they named the level plain Llano Estacada. (Courtesy *Hobbs News-Sun*.)

ON THE COVER: The Lea County sheriff's posse leads the 1941 Fourth of July Parade down the 200 block of West Broadway in Hobbs, New Mexico. (Courtesy Jim Rawls.)

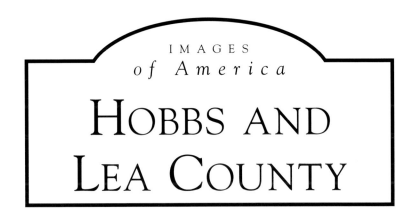

HOBBS AND LEA COUNTY

IMAGES of America

Max A. Clampitt

Copyright © 2008 by Max A. Clampitt
ISBN 978-0-7385-5856-1

Published by Arcadia Publishing
Charleston SC, Chicago IL, Portsmouth NH, San Francisco CA

Printed in the United States of America

Library of Congress Catalog Card Number: 2008932137

For all general information contact Arcadia Publishing at:
Telephone 843-853-2070
Fax 843-853-0044
E-mail sales@arcadiapublishing.com
For customer service and orders:
Toll-Free 1-888-313-2665

Visit us on the Internet at www.arcadiapublishing.com

*To Wilma M. Clampitt, for her assistance and support in this endeavor,
and to all of the pioneer ranchers, farmers, cavalry soldiers, and
homesteaders who came to the New Mexico Territory and
New Mexico State to contribute so much
to its vibrant cultures and rich history.*

Contents

Acknowledgments		6
Introduction		7
1.	Buffalo Hunters and Cavalry Expeditions	11
2.	Homesteaders, Ranches, Railroads, and the Discovery of Oil	17
3.	A Town Is Born	25
4.	Boomtowns, the Great Depression, and World War II	67
5.	Economic Development	99
About the Author		127

ACKNOWLEDGMENTS

In writing this book and choosing the title, *Hobbs and Lea County*, I have taken a very special trip down memory lane. I have been writing a history column each Sunday in the *Hobbs News-Sun*, beginning on October 15, 1998. As I started interviewing some of the pioneers in this area, reading magazines and newspaper clippings, and looking at hundreds of old photographs, I became aware of the urgent need to, in some way, help preserve as much as I could of the growth and history of the New Mexico Territory and Lea County.

I was 13 yeas old in 1937 when my family moved to Lea County, so I do not consider myself to be a true pioneer, but over the years, I have visited with many of the people who came to this area or were born here around the dawn of the 20th century. Many of my readers have encouraged me to write a book, so when I was contacted by Jared Jackson, an acquisitions editor for Arcadia Publishing, I decided to get to work on it. My special thanks go to Jared for his assistance on the layout and for patiently answering my many questions.

I owe a special debt of gratitude to several people who have encouraged me to use my newspaper columns and photographs to write this book. There is Mary Lyle, Brenda Brooks, Mildred Lasley, Jim Harris, Ray Battaglini, Joe Byers, Wade Shipley, Johnny Burgess, Sylvia Petterson, and others too numerous to mention. Of course, there is my wife, Wilma, who serves faithfully as my best critic and proofreader. Also, I had the strong support of my son, Mike Clampitt, and my daughter, Donna Hooten.

INTRODUCTION

Lea County and its several towns are blessed with a colorful history and a rich heritage. Although this part of the United States is quite a distance from the rest of the nation, there is much to remember and record about its growth and development during the past 150 years. A few towns, such as Santa Fe and Las Cruces, date as far back as the 16th and 17th centuries. Most of the rest of New Mexico was sparsely populated by several Native American tribes and some Mexican families who migrated to the northern part of the state.

Several Native American tribes occupied the Lea County section of New Mexico territory simply as a hunting ground, especially when they became aware that it was home to the last of the huge buffalo herds. Buffalo furnished natives with food, clothing, and material with which to build shelter.

When this part of North America was controlled by Spain, several expeditions explored the area. There were some strong beliefs that there were "Seven Cities of Gold" somewhere north of Mexico, but they were never found. However, these expeditions documented several detailed charts and records of their findings.

In October 1849, the U.S. Army sent a caravan of 18 wagons commanded by Capt. Randolph B. Marcy, with orders to check out the southeast quarter of New Mexico Territory. Captain Marcy pictured Santa Fe as "a miserable group of low, flat houses all huddled together inside a mud wall." But the government was especially interested in finding a good place to bring the transcontinental railroad farther west and on to California. Since trains needed a good supply of watering stations for their steam-powered engines, the New Mexico Territory simply did not meet this all-important requirement. So over the ensuing years, this part of the county became known as a high, dry desert all the way from West Texas to the Pecos River. The railroad was forced to follow the 32nd Parallel, about 80 miles south of New Mexico's southern border.

In the 1870s, several more scouting details were dispatched from Fort Concho, near San Angelo, Texas. One such expedition was a regiment of black soldiers, led by William Rufus Shafter. They discovered Monument Springs a few miles southwest of present-day Hobbs. Gen. Nelson Miles and Capt. Nichols Nolan led a cavalry group that was successful in capturing probably the last renegade band of Native Americans at Dug Springs, a few miles south of Monument. Captain Nolan's mission became known as the Forlorn Hope Expedition because of poor planning and preparation. He lost all of his horses, four of his men died, and all of the rest were disabled. A few men deserted and made their way back to water across the Texas border near present-day Lubbock, Texas. A Texas Ranger named G. W. Arrington led a scouting party into what is now the northern part of Lea County in 1879; there were mostly saline lakes with a few springs around them.

When the last of the huge buffalo herds were killed off, most of the buffalo hunters left the county. However, two of them, Jim Harvey and Dick Wilkerson, decided to stay. They had learned from the Native Americans that water could be found by digging 6 to 8 feet down in some of the draws and low places, so they decided to dig a well, lay claim to it, and sell it to newcomers in the territory. This was all in the south part of what is now Lea County.

Two other ex-hunters were Thomas L. "George" Causey and George Jefferson. They stayed on and began ranching in the northern part of this county. This was around the Ranger Lake and the Four Lakes area. In addition to raising cattle, they also were rounding up and breaking herds of wild mustangs in 1882.

So it was this region, known as mostly a high and dry desert, to which homesteaders were drawn in search of new beginnings and free land under the Homestead Act passed by Congress.

The Homestead Act allowed people to move to West Texas and the New Mexico Territory, file on 160 acres, live on it for three years and make improvements, and then the land was theirs. So the invasion of open-range cattle country was not made by military means but by the creaking wagons with loads of household goods, farming tools, and families seeking a better life.

Along with the ranch buildings, present at that time were a windmill and a stock tank with some cottonwood trees around it. From a distance, these clumps of trees and buildings looked like small islands in a sea of gramma grass and mesquite bushes. To the travelers scanning the horizon while riding a long, dry, dusty trail in the heat, these distant ghostly islands called out a promise of water, shade, and neighborly fellowship. At sundown, those distant clumps of trees offered the hope of a bed and a meal, as well as rest for the horses. This country became known for its hospitality and warm welcome. Even if locals did not know these travelers, it was common courtesy to welcome newcomers. After all, they would probably soon become new friends and neighbors.

James Isaac Hobbs died in 1923, so, of course, he never had any idea how his homestead was destined to change into the thriving city it is today or that this city would bear his name. His widow, Frances, lived to see the area change and became known as "Grandma Hobbs" all over the county. The town honored her in many ways. She was enthusiastic, loyal, and proud of "her town" for the rest of her life.

A few years earlier, rancher Col. R. S. "Old General" MacKenzie had moved into the Monument area and brought his string of cattle, branded with the "Dumb Bell" brand. About the same time, two more ranches were started south and southeast of Monument Springs, and were operated by Jim Daughtery and Fran Divers, respectively. Then Claiborne Walker Merchant and his son John Merchant brought in a large herd from their San Simon Ranch in the eastern Arizona Territory. Jim Campbell set up the High Lonesome Ranch along the Texas state line, bringing a large herd and digging two fine wells. On the western side of the territory, the Turkey Track Ranch was started on the east bank of the Pecos River. Cape Willingham was the manager and the first to explore two springs at the base of the Mescalero Escarpment, sometimes called the "Caprock." George Causey followed the last buffalo herd and is said to have killed the last buffalo in this area. He stayed and started raising mustangs as well as cattle on his Four Lakes Ranch. In a few years, he sold his ranch to "Major" George W. Littlefield, who changed the ranch name to L. F. D., a derivative of Littlefield Freight Drivers.

Early on, ranchers had little trouble with "squatters," but when the Homestead Act was passed in May 1862, some problems arose. One incident concerns a man who squatted near a seep below the Caprock on the Tunnels Ranch, which was owned by Joe Allen Browning. He made it clear he intended to stay. Warned to move, he refused and even took a shot at some of the "Tunnel" cowboys. Browning decided to take action, so he rode over and politely asked the man to leave. The man told him that he had the government behind him, so Browning told him that was just fine: "You get the government here in the next fifteen minutes to take over. If you don't have all of your junk in your wagon and moving over that hill by that time, there won't be anything left to move." The squatter was packed up and gone in 10 minutes, never to be seen again.

Soon the town of Hobbs began to grow. James Isaac Hobbs wanted to proceed on northwest to the Estancia Valley, but his kinfolk talked him into filing on a homestead near theirs. His homestead was for 320 acres in what is currently the southeast part of the city of Hobbs. For several months, family members lived in their two wagons and a large dugout they managed to construct nearby. Hobbs noticed an almost miraculous improvement in the health of his wife and son, so he totally gave up any further thoughts of going on to Estancia and dug a well and set up a windmill. Then he made two long cross-country trips to Midland, Texas, for lumber to build a little two-room house next to the dugout.

The isolation of the Hobbs family was short-lived because 1908 and 1909 saw a flood of wagons and families come into the area. Soon there were nearly 50 homesteads within a few hours' ride of them. This impressed Hobbs to visit people across the area, soliciting money to help build a schoolhouse. Folks were excited about the project, and in a few months, a 16-by-24-foot frame structure was built, serving as a schoolhouse, dance hall, church, and a play theater. The year 1909 saw 42 students attending school for a three-month term.

At that time, everything not grown in little family gardens had to be brought in by wagon from either Carlsbad or Midland, a five- or six-day trip in either direction. Supplies that early homesteaders needed included groceries, dry goods, coal oil, lumber, and so forth. In 1909, James Isaac Hobbs helped his son James Berry Hobbs establish the first general mercantile store to serve the local community. James Berry, now 20 years old, lived in the back of the store building.

Later that same year, James Berry Hobbs circulated a petition to the U.S. Postal Department for a post office. At this time, the government required that before a post office could be authorized, the applicant must have carried the mail from the nearest postal facility for a period of three months without pay. In 1909, the nearest postal facility was at Monument, about 10 miles southwest of Berry's Store. The application form required a suggestion of three names for the proposed office. The names Prairie View, Taft, and Loving were proposed, but for some unknown reason, the officials in Washington must have liked the signature of James Berry Hobbs on the application, and the name Hobbs was chosen. James Berry Hobbs became the unofficial first postmaster, and his general merchandise store became known as the Hobbs Store and Post Office. This post office was not actually established until May 7, 1909, and George W. Rogers was appointed the official first postmaster on January 26, 1910.

In the 1920s, the town began to boom as the Midwest Refining Company sent its Roswell manager to Hobbs to select a drilling site for an oil well. It was to be an exploratory ("wildcat") well. Manager Ronald K. Deford chose a spot about a mile southwest of the little store and windmill, on the Will Terry Ranch. A crew of men came in, erected a wooden drilling rig, and started work. After a few weeks, the rig caught fire and was shut down. A steel derrick was brought in from Tucumcari, more than 100 miles north, over country that had few roads. Several months later, the new rig was up and running, and on June 13, 1928, the well came in as a "gusher," producing some 800 barrels of oil per day. But there was another delay.

The well had to be shut down again because there were no pipelines, and storage tanks had to be installed. The nearest railroad was about 65 miles south, and there were few roads to handle truck traffic. By 1929, most of these problems had been fixed or at least were showing progress. Meanwhile, early in January 1930, the Humble Oil and Refining Company had completed its Bowers Number 1-A in the Hobbs field, and tests showed there was a whopping potential of 9,720 barrels per day. Word spread at once throughout the oil industry, and another influx of workers appeared on the scene, coming from Oklahoma, Kansas, and Texas. The skyline was fast becoming covered with oil derricks in every direction, as well as oil tank batteries and gas flares casting their bright lights into the night sky.

The Great Depression caused many of the stores and business buildings to be abandoned in Hobbs. Many of these structures were prey to thieves and "daylight burglars." Sometimes an old boy would just back up to a small house, run a part of skids under the floor-joists, and haul it away, occasionally even to one of the neighboring towns. A story is told about one man who ran a bakery here. He and his family encountered a truck and trailer with a house loaded on it, headed for Carlsbad. He turned to his wife and called out, "By Golly, that looked like our house!" His wife agreed, and they turned around, chased down the truck, stopped it, and made the driver take it back to Hobbs. Many of the houses built in the early 1930s were called "shotgun houses" because a shotgun could be fired through the front door and the shot would go out the back door and never hit a thing inside the house. Also most of these houses were built with sheetrock and two-by-fours with no kind of sheeting on the outside.

None of the streets or highways were paved in Lea County until after 1937, when the economy began to recover. World War II helped. Construction was started at once on the Hobbs Army Air Base Field and progressed so fast that the field was officially open for training in late July 1942.

The first A-20 Avenger twin-engine bombardier training airplanes arrived in September 1942. A few months later, a squadron of B-17 four-engine Flying Fortress bombers arrived and started training.

During the construction period, there were many contractors and workers pouring into the city. They were followed immediately by approximately 5,900 civilian and army personnel. The housing situation became acute in Hobbs, and many residents opened up their spare bedrooms, garage apartments, and any available space to accommodate these newcomers.

When the war was over Europe in May 1945, the training program was curtailed, and the base was placed on inactive status. Then it was turned into a storage depot. There were some 1,600 P-51 fighter airplanes and A-26 attack bombers flown in from all over the world. These airplanes were lined up and down on both sides of all four runways, tied down, and then "pickled" for protection against rain and sandstorms.

One year later, orders came down to take the airplanes out of storage and transfer them to other bases. The base, covering more than 2,700 acres, was shuffled around through other designations and finally was turned over to the War Assets Administration. It was at last given to the City of Hobbs by quit claim deed effective October 12, 1956.

At present, economic development has risen in Hobbs, with approximately 2,200 vacancies that employers are seeking to fill. Lea County and the surrounding areas are today areas of labor shortages. Everyone who wants to work is already working. Efforts to attract and recruit suitable workers, especially those with education, skills, and experience, are seriously hampered by the lack of available housing. Several large housing projects are underway, but the progress is slow because of the worker shortage.

Government agencies, the chamber of commerce, and the Lea County Economic Development Corporation are currently going all-out to attract new, diversified businesses and having great success. Beautification is also being stressed, which is helping to make Hobbs look less like an old-time "oil boom" town. City parks and other recreational facilities are being updated and enlarged to bring Hobbs into economic stability.

One

BUFFALO HUNTERS AND CAVALRY EXPEDITIONS

Capt. John Pope was dispatched to the Southwest by Secretary of the Army Jefferson Davis shortly after the end of the Civil War in perhaps the first major army expedition into New Mexico Territory. The expedition began on the Texas Gulf Coast port of Indianola, covering 500 miles; their assignment was to search for artesian water wells for the construction of the transcontinental railroad.

Captain Pope set up a base in the New Mexico Territory east of the Pecos River. Able to find water at 360 feet, the pumps could not lift the water, and without casing, the well caved in and was abandoned. Pope's expedition was a failure.

During the 1860s, tensions between natives and the westward movement of cattlemen, farmers, and homesteaders increased dramatically. Army expeditions were dispatched from Fort Davis and Fort Concho, near San Angelo, Texas. On patrol, Capt. Nicolas Nolan was defeated by poor leadership, bad luck, and inexperience. Two buffalo hunters warned Nolan of the "point of no return" as far as water was concerned, but Nolan pressed on and lost nearly half his men and horses on a little sand hill near the Caprock in present-day Lea County.

Col. R. S. MacKenzie of Civil War fame crossed the present Lea County area several times with troops from the 10th Cavalry Regiment, comprised nearly entirely of veterans of the Civil War. Natives called them "Buffalo Soldiers" in reference to their black, curly hair.

Shafter Lake, just across the state line in Texas, bears the name of Maj. Gen. William R. Shafter. On one of his expeditions in the territory, he camped for a time at Monument Spring, about 15 miles southwest of Hobbs. The spring was the only known source of water in this area. General Shafter had his men build a huge pile of caliche rocks on a small rise southwest of the spring. This is how the village of Monument received its name. The pile of rocks could be seen for great distances, helping those traveling through this area find water.

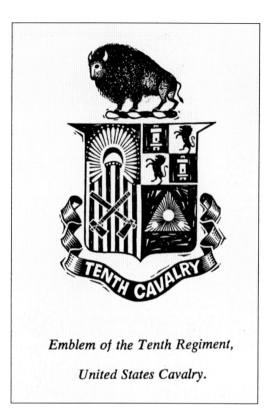

Emblem of the Tenth Regiment, United States Cavalry.

This emblem was designed for the Buffalo Soldiers, the 10th Regiment of the U.S. Cavalry. (Courtesy National Archives.)

Several illustrations were created of the Buffalo Soldiers, such as this one dating to December 1886, which shows a 10th Regiment, U.S. Cavalry outing from Fort Concho in San Angelo, Texas. (Courtesy National Archives.)

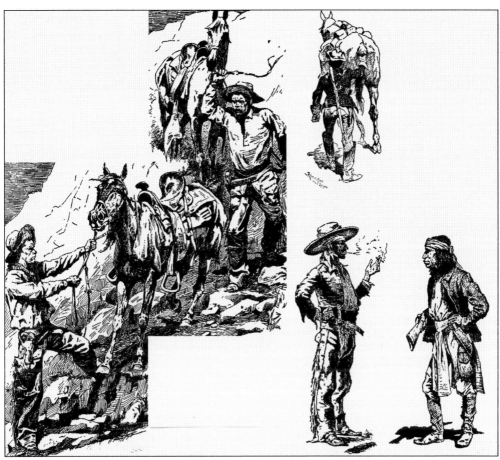

An array of illustrations was created for the Buffalo Soldiers, 10th Regiment, U.S. Cavalry, between the years 1886 and 1889. (Courtesy National Archives.)

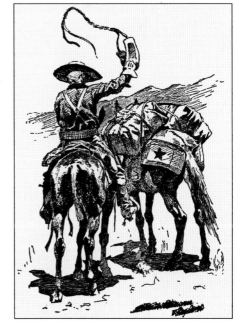

Mules carried the equipment and supplies for the Buffalo Soldiers' outing from Fort Davis, Texas, in December 1886 (right). (Courtesy National Archives.)

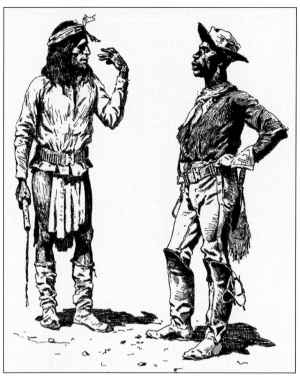

Black soldiers traded with and were assisted in navigating the terrain by Apache soldiers or scouts. Here is a 10th Regiment of the U.S. Cavalry outing in December 1886. (Courtesy National Archives.)

The depiction below illustrates the tools and equipment used by the Buffalo Soldiers, 10th Regiment, in December 1886. (Courtesy National Archives.)

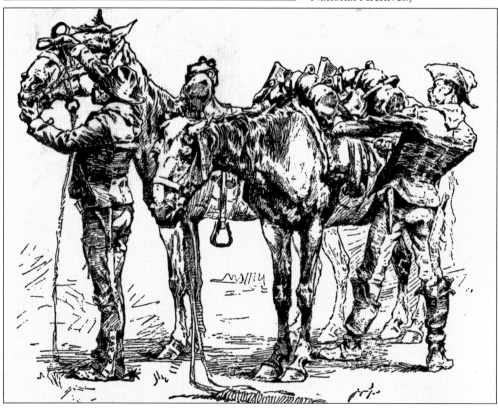

Soldiers in the 10th Regiment of the U.S. Cavalry would ride horses to navigate the terrain in Lea County. (Courtesy National Archives.)

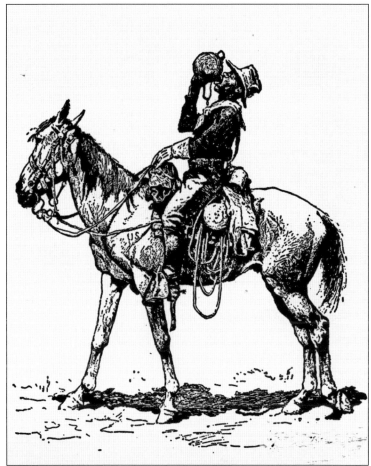

In 1886, the Buffalo Soldiers of the 10th Regiment served as protection against Native Americans. These officers (below) were stationed at Fort Davis, New Mexico. (Courtesy *Hobbs News-Sun*.)

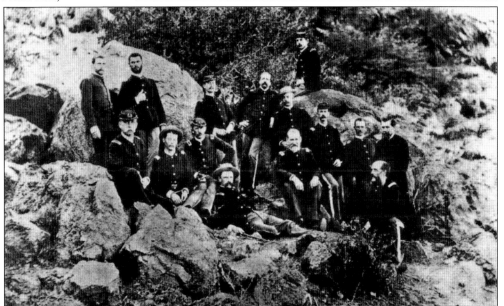

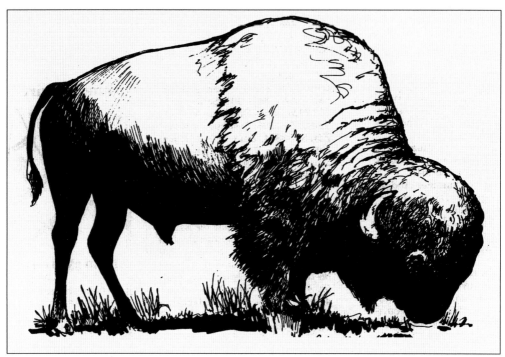
The iconic buffalo was illustrated for promotional purposes to recruit new soldiers into the Buffalo Soldiers' 10th Regiment of the U.S. Cavalry in December 1886. (Courtesy National Archives.)

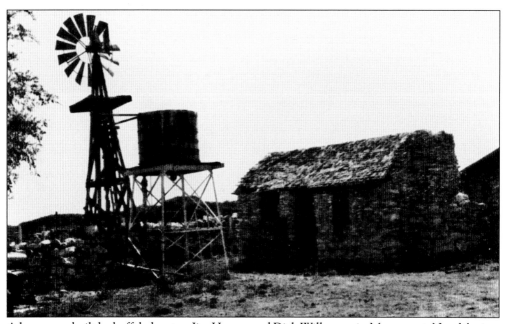
A house was built by buffalo hunters Jim Harvey and Dick Wilkerson in Monument, New Mexico, in 1875. (Courtesy Naomi Houge.)

Two

Homesteaders, Ranches, Railroads, and the Discovery of Oil

In their seemingly short history, Lea County and the city of Hobbs experienced two major changes that would shape their future. The first one began in the early 1900s, when Congress passed the Homestead Act and a slow but steady surge of folks started moving into this part of the New Mexico Territory. The second major change took place in 1927 and 1928 when oil was discovered.

In 1879, pioneers migrated to the New Mexico Territory. Previously, buffalo hunters worked on the last big herd of buffalo in the United States. Army cavalries launched several expeditions that chased natives and searched for significant streams or bodies of water. For many years, this territory was recognized as strictly a "high desert," but the hunters and cavalry reported "grass belly deep to a horse," so a few cattlemen moved and tried their luck ranching.

One of the first ranchers was J. A. Browning in 1885. Browning scouted the area with his large herd of cattle and built a house out of caliche rocks. He also constructed a large dugout near the Texas line.

As the oil boom rushed into its third year, tank batteries were going up all over the area, and hundreds of pipelines were being laid to transport oil as well as natural gas. The problem was getting this product to market.

A great deal of relief took place as carloads of people met the Texas–New Mexico Railway, which stopped at Jal, Eunice, and Hobbs, then went on to Lovington. Bands and flag wavers greeted the train at every stop; the happy day was April 19, 1930. New Mexico governor Richard C. Dillon was at the throttle, along with a large detail of state officials and railroad VIPs.

Passenger service was stopped during the Great Depression but resumed in early 1942 as the Hobbs Army Air Field began operation and the first of nearly 4,000 airmen arrived. Passenger service stopped again when the air base was closed in the late 1940s. The Texas–New Mexico Railway is still in business, moving fuel and building materials from the Navajo Refinery, located north of Hobbs.

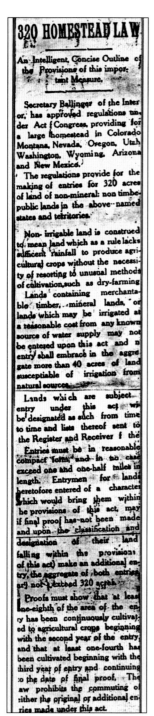

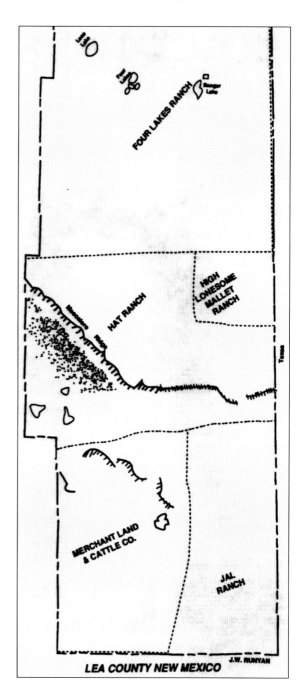

An article about the 320 Homestead Law boasts of an intelligent, concise outline of the provisions of the important measure (left). Proofs showed that one-eighth of the land had been continuously cultivated to agricultural crops. The law prohibited the commuting of either the original or additional lands made under this act. (Courtesy *Lovington Leader*.)

Maps were drawn up to illustrate the divisions of the five major ranches in the future Lea County (right). (Courtesy J. W. Runyan.)

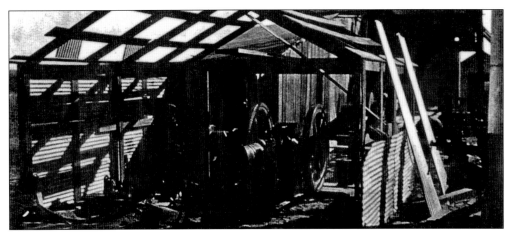

This rig was under construction in the fall of 1925, as a sheet-iron structure is being erected around the power plant. It was located just south of the village of Maljamar. (Courtesy Kenneth Shields.)

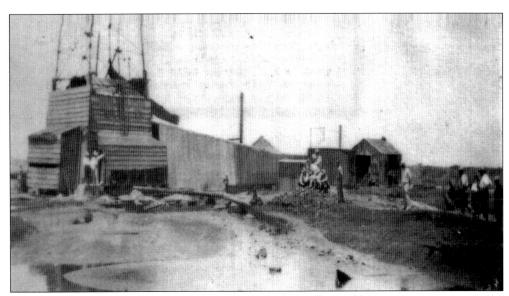

In 1928, oil was discovered with a cable tool rig, which was finished by a steam rotary rig, on the Will Terry Ranch at the corner of South Grimes Street and Stanolind Road at the Discovery Well for Hobbs Field. (Courtesy Kenneth Shields.)

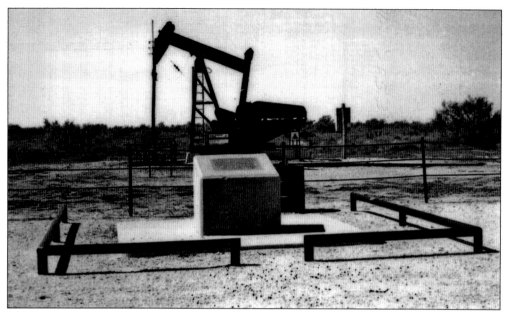
The Discovery Well, located on the corner of South Grimes Street and Stanolind Road, produced oil until 2003. This photograph was taken in 1973. (Courtesy Kenneth Shields.)

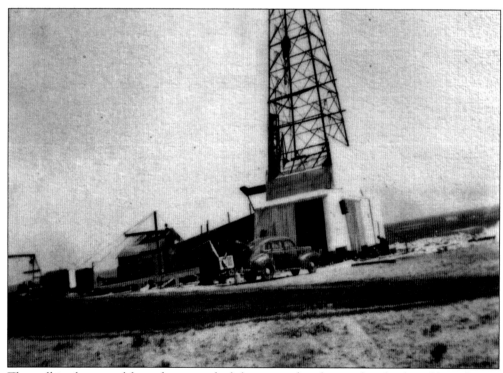
The walking beam and forge shown on the left were used to sharpen bits for the cable tool rig in 1935. (Courtesy Kenneth Shields.)

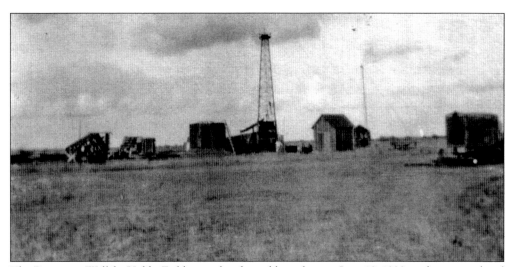

The Discovery Well for Hobbs Field started with a cable tool rig on June 13, 1928, and was completed by November 8, 1928, with a steam rotary rig. The well site at South Grimes and Stanolind Road was on land leased from the Will Terry Ranch. (Courtesy Ed Seabourne.)

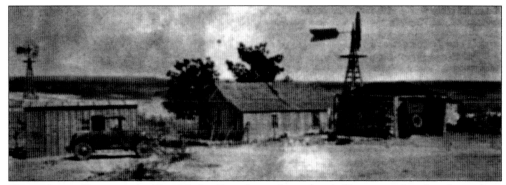

Home Sweet Home at the Dru Taylor Ranch is where the drilling crew lived and ate their meals. Their sleeping quarters were in the small building to the left, which was constructed for this purpose. A larger rooming house for oil-field workers was later built nearby. (Courtesy Kenneth Shields.)

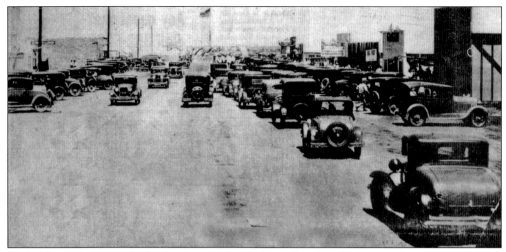

Main Street in New Hobbs is pictured in 1930 on the day the first train came to Hobbs. Mrs. B. C. Petty said the Petty family lived behind the first building on the right, which was a café. She recalled open gambling taking place in the café, and often there were thousands of dollars to be seen on the table. She also recalled seeing gamblers carry thousands away in sacks. (Courtesy Ed Seabourne.)

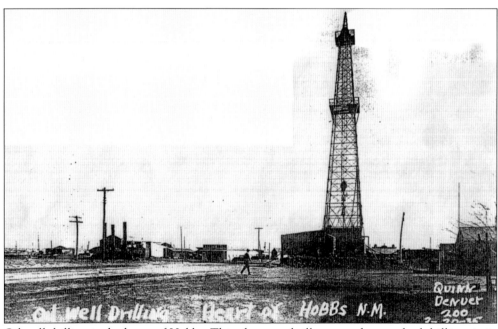

Oil-well drilling is the heart of Hobbs. This photograph illustrates the standard drilling rig in 1935, at a location just south of the 500 block of West Broadway. (Courtesy Ed Seabourne.)

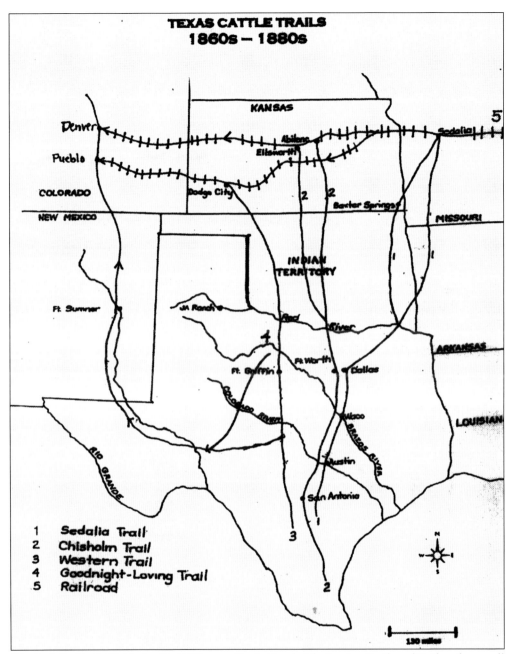

The Sedalia Trail, Chisholm Trail, Western Trail, Goodnight-Loving Trail, and Railroad were all used as part of the Texas cattle trails from the 1860s to the 1880s. (Courtesy Hobbs Library.)

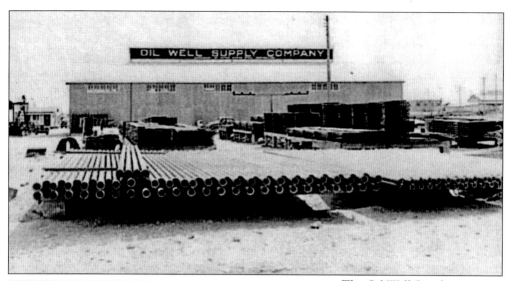

The Oil Well Supply Company (above) was located in the 700 block of West Broadway in 1936. (Courtesy Ed Seabourne.)

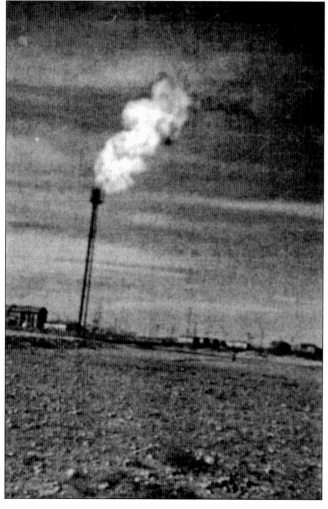

The Hobbs Flare was a longtime landmark located at 1625 West Marland Boulevard. The flare was first installed in 1930 by Phillips Oil. (Courtesy Ed Seabourne.)

Three

A Town Is Born

James Isaac Hobbs left his home in the farming community of Brown County, Texas, in the fall of 1906 with his wife, Frances, and four of his children. Hobbs loaded his two wagons and set out for Alpine, Texas. His wife and one of his sons had a respiratory problem, and Hobbs felt a higher, drier climate would be beneficial to them. He had also heard that good homesteads were available on the western frontier.

The winter caught the Hobbs family in Coleman, Texas, so they spent the winter picking cotton before resuming their journey. Somewhere short of the Texas–New Mexico Territory boundary, they met another family in a wagon heading in the opposite direction. Stopping for a brief conversation, the Hobbses told the eastbound man they were heading for Alpine, and the man promptly replied, "Do not go to that God-forsaken place! We just left there, and we simply could not make a living there!" So Hobbs thought it over for a little while and decided to change his course and head for the New Mexico Territory. New Mexico did not become a state until 1912. After a journey of almost seven months, they crossed over the Texas line. After about five miles more, they stopped to rest and visit one of their relatives who was homesteading.

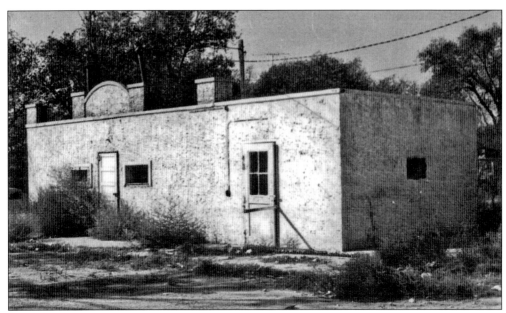
The New Hobbs Jail was built in 1930 in the 900 block of South Dal Paso Street. (Courtesy *Lovington Leader*.)

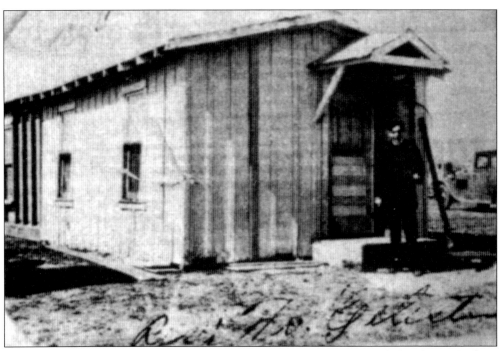
Father Celistine is shown standing in front of the first St. Helena Catholic church built in Hobbs. It was located on the corner of the property where Marian Hall is now located on East Main Street. Father Celistine came from Carlsbad to hold Mass for the first Catholic residents of Hobbs, and Catholics from all over the county came here once a week when he made the trip. (Courtesy *Lovington Leader*.)

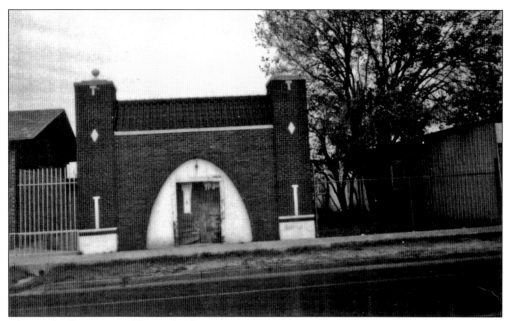

The city hall in New Hobbs was built in 1929 on 306 East Main Street. The building was donated to the Salvation Army in 1937 when two town site companies, "Old Hobbs" and "New Hobbs," merged. (Courtesy Max Clampitt.)

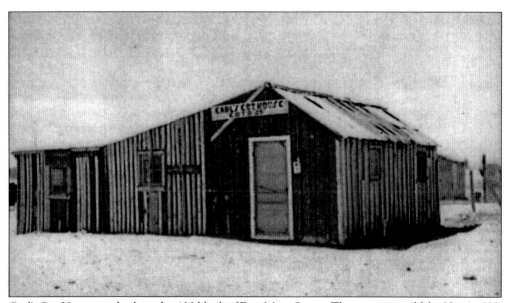

Carl's Cot House was built in the 400 block of East Main Street. The cots were sold for 35¢ in 1929. (Courtesy Ed Seabourne.)

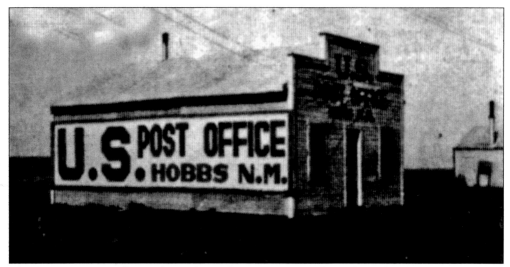

The first U.S. Post Office is shown here after it was moved from the Hobbs family store. It was located on East Main Street close to Marian Hall. New Hobbs was a town of its own until it was consolidated with Hobbs in 1938. (Courtesy *Hobbs Flare*.)

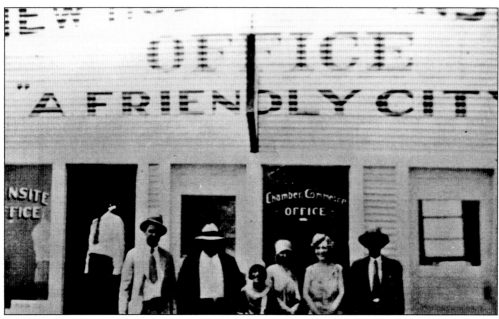

In 1930, the New Hobbs town site office was located in the 300 block of East Main Street. (Courtesy *Hobbs Flare*.)

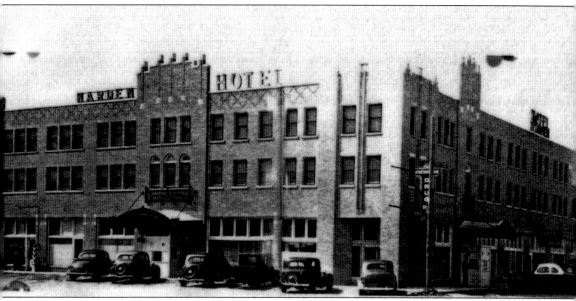

Built in 1930, the Harden Hotel, located on the corner of Main and Houston Streets, had a barbershop, drugstore, and café. It also had the only elevator in Hobbs in 1935. The Harden cost nearly $200,000 to build and was condemned in 1974. (Courtesy *Hobbs Flare*.)

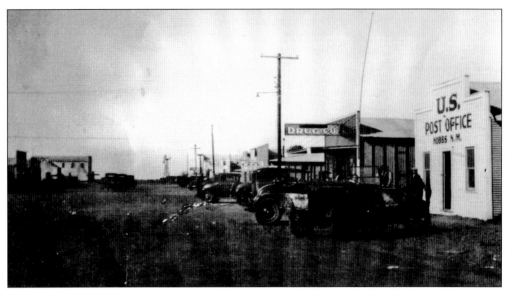

This photograph was taken facing west at the intersection of Main and Dal Paso Streets in 1929. (Courtesy Lois Troutt.)

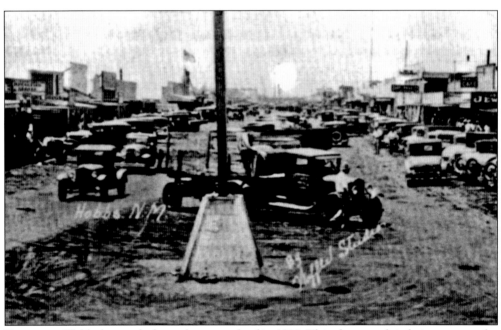

Downtown Hobbs boomed when oil was struck oil in 1930. This photograph is facing west on the corner of Dalmont Street and the 100 block of East Carlsbad Street (later known as Broadway). (Courtesy Lois Troutt.)

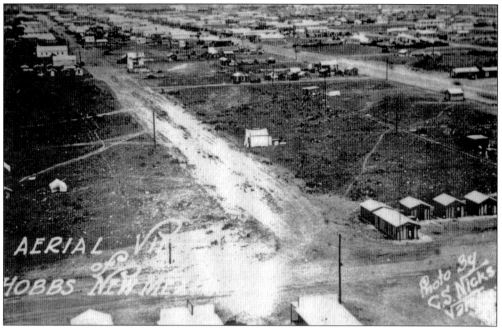

This c. 1930 aerial photograph shows Hobbs in its formative period. Above is Broadway Street looking west, and below is Dal Paso Street looking north. (Courtesy Lois Troutt.)

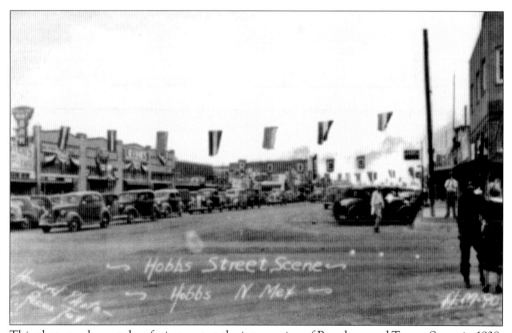

This photograph was taken facing west at the intersection of Broadway and Turner Street in 1938. (Courtesy Lois Troutt.)

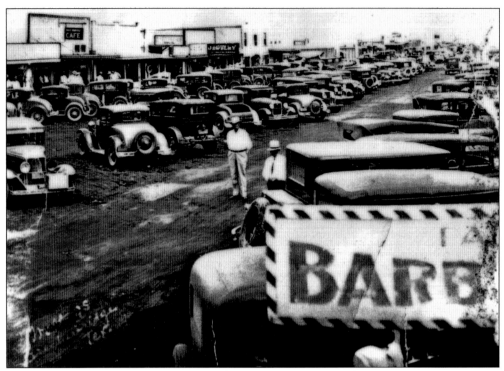

This photograph was taken facing west on the 100 block of East Carlsbad Street in 1930. (Courtesy Lois Troutt.)

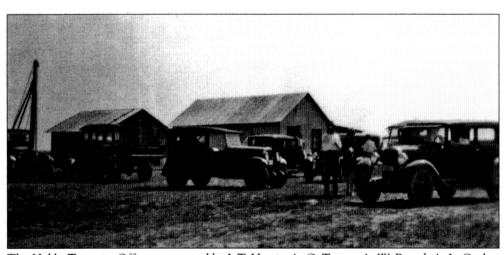

The Hobbs Townsite Office was owned by J. T. Harris, A. G. Troutt, A. W. Board, A. L. Gurley, and J. J. Carson. The office was located on 101 East Carlsbad Street (later known as Broadway) in 1928. (Courtesy Lois Troutt.)

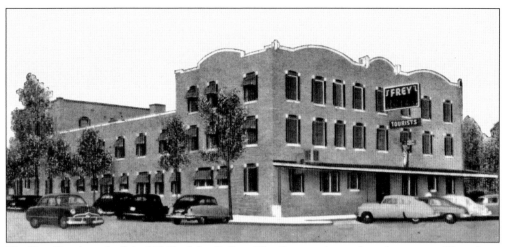

The Frey Hotel was built in 1936 by John B. Frey. The Frey was located on the corner of Broadway and Folwer Street and was demolished in 1977. (Courtesy Lois Troutt.)

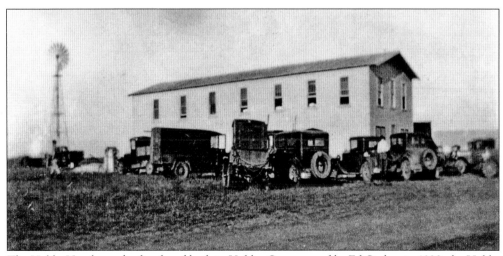

The Hobbs Hotel was the first hotel built in Hobbs. Constructed by Ed Cathey in 1928, the Hobbs was located at the intersection of Broadway and Turner Street. (Courtesy Lois Troutt.)

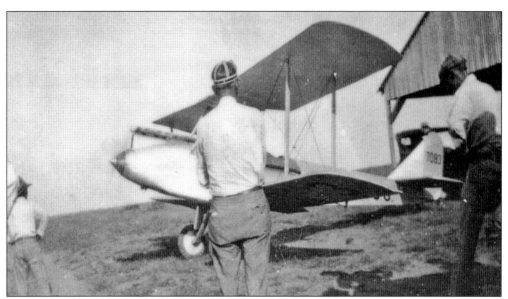

Amelia Earhart's airplane landed on East Carlsbad Street in late September 1928. She was lost on a solo round-trip across the United States. Her airplane was a 1927 model Aviro-Avian. She made a telephone call and sent a telegram from the Hobbs Hotel, which also had the only telephone in town. (Courtesy Lois Troutt.)

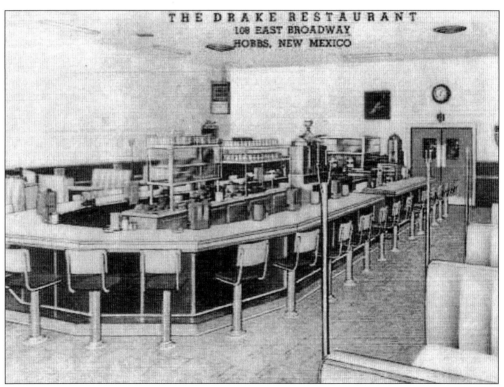

The Drake Restaurant, located at 108 East Broadway, was later remodeled and changed into the Drake Café. (Courtesy Lois Troutt.)

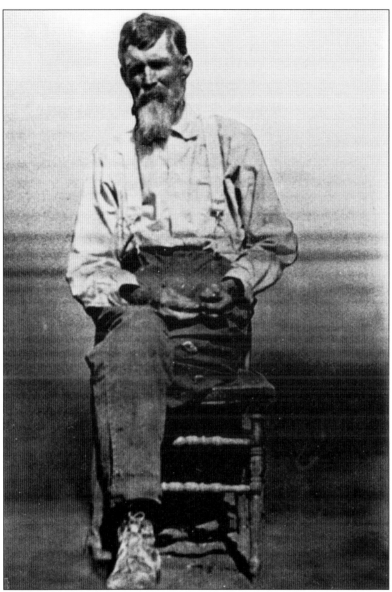

James Isaac Hobbs was born January 3, 1854, at Cornith, Mississippi. His father, Berry Hobbs, volunteered for service in the Confederate army, from which he never retuned. James Isaac had to make his own way in the world from the early age of 8. By the age of 20, he arrived in Texas, locating near Point, Texas, in Rains County. Here he met and married Frances Mooring on December 13, 1877. Frances was the daughter of Dr. John Ellis Mooring, a noted and widely known personage of this country in those days. To this union, there was born eight children. The remainder of Hobbs's life was spent on the frontier of Texas and in New Mexico; he was always moving westward as the line of settlements advanced. He moved his family to Brown County, Texas, in 1885, but his wife and son were not healthy, and a doctor suggested he move them to a higher, dryer climate. He loaded his family and belongings into two covered wagons and started west again in the fall of 1906. In April 1907, they reached New Mexico Territory and settled on what was then un-surveyed public domain land in eastern Eddy County. (Courtesy Ernest Byers.)

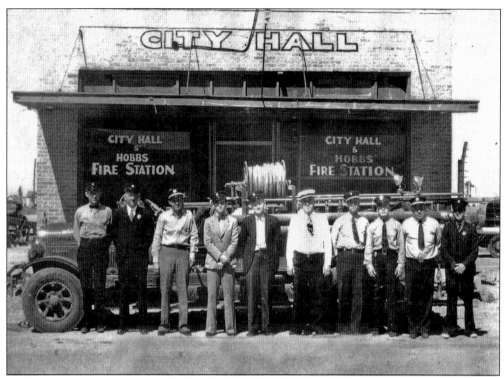

There were 10 members of the Hobbs Volunteer Fire Department in 1936. From left to right are O. J. Barnes, Dan E. Lake, S. S. Blakeley, Jessie Hennsie, Spencer Borgen, Floyd Wynn, Early Strawn, Frank Barmettler, Leo Conner, and Pete Gotcher. The fire engine is a 1930 model Seagrave Pumper, the first in Hobbs. (Courtesy Lois Troutt.)

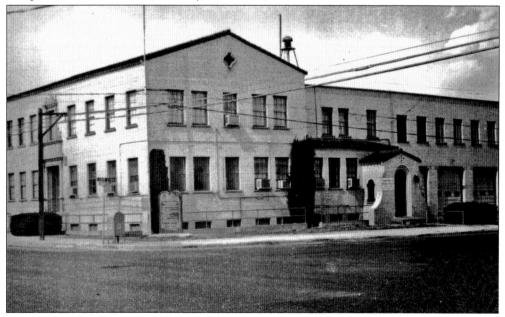

The Hobbs City Hall was built in 1939 on the corner of North Turner and East Cain Streets. The city hall was remodeled in 1984. (Courtesy Lois Troutt.)

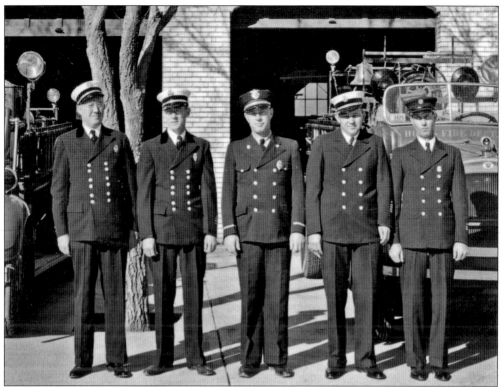

The Hobbs Fire Department officers are, from left to right, Chief Dan E. Lake, Herman Copp, Floyd Wynn, S. S. Blakeley, and Charles Gregory. They pose next to two fire trucks—the GMC ("Jimmy") and Seagrave ("Mandy")—in the 100 block of East Cain Street on the south side of city hall in 1944. (Courtesy Hobbs Fire Department.)

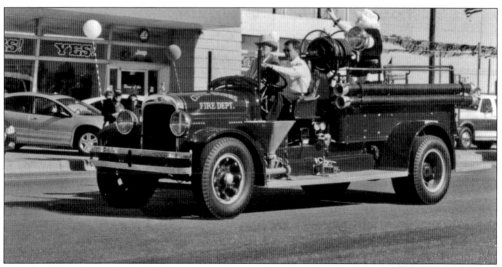

Old No. 5, the 1930 model Seagrave pumper, is featured in the 1998 Christmas Parade in Hobbs. The driver is Lt. Ray DuPlessis, and the passenger is Cliff Lasley (wearing the cowboy hat), who was Hobbs's second fire chief. (Courtesy Hobbs Fire Department.)

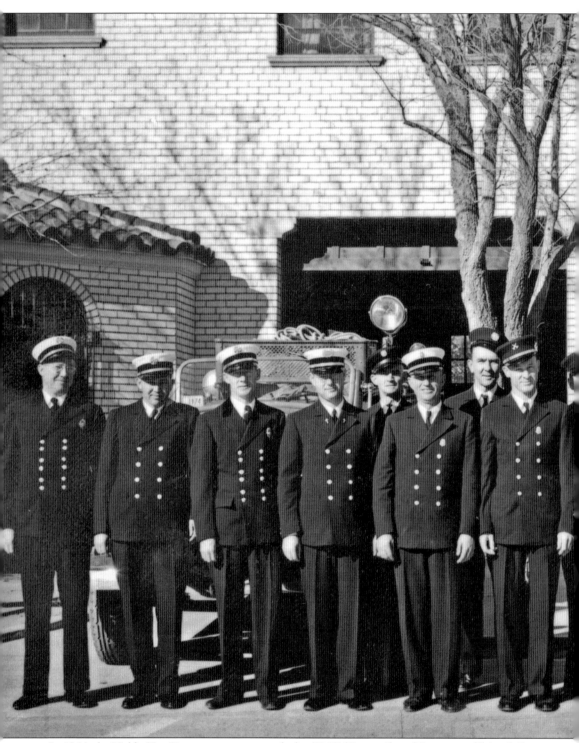

In 1944, the Hobbs Fire Department poses with the GMC ("Jimmy") and Seagraves ("Mandy") on East Cain Street at the side of city hall. From left to right are Chief Dan E. Lake; Shirley Blakeley; Herman Coppedge; chaplin Roy Davis; M. L. Bufkin; Harry King; C. M. Sullins; Oscar Shaw;

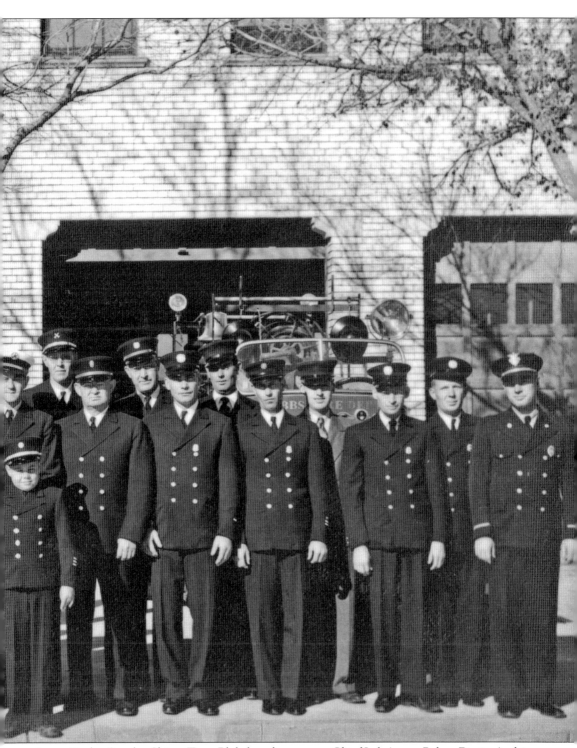

James Drake; Stanley Shipp; Terry Blakeley; the mascot, Chief Lake's son; Belver Davis; Archie Conner; Denver Shaw; J. E. Jackson; Bill Hibon; Charley Gregory; J. E. Cotton; J. D. Heath; Jack Wilder; and Floyd Wynn. (Courtesy Hobbs Fire Department.)

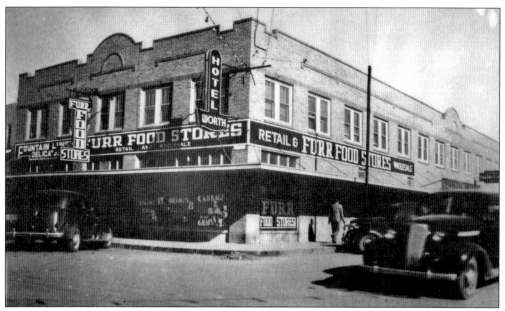

The Furr Food Store, located at the intersection of West Broadway and Shipp Street, featured the Worth Hotel on the top floor. (Courtesy Lois Troutt.)

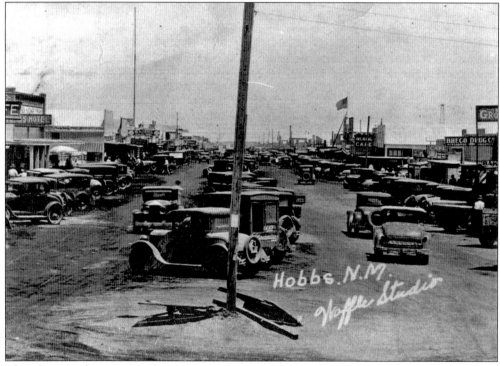

This photograph was taken facing east at the intersection of Linam Street and West Broadway in 1930. (Courtesy Lois Troutt.)

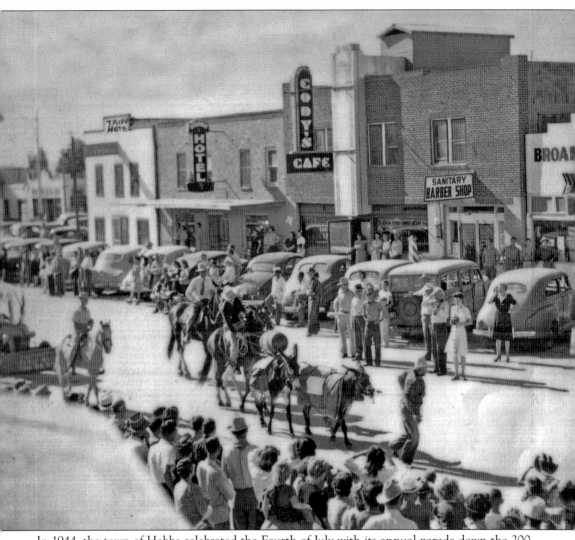

In 1944, the town of Hobbs celebrated the Fourth of July with its annual parade down the 200 block of West Broadway. (Courtesy *Hobbs News-Sun*.)

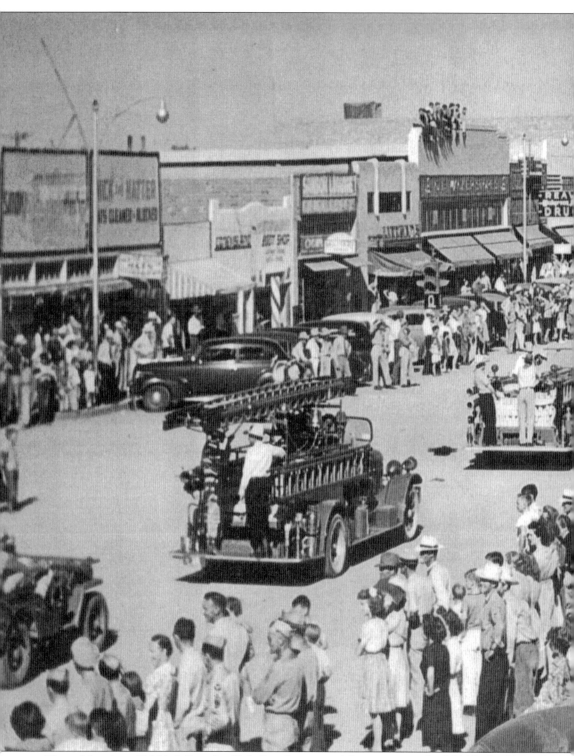

The celebration of Hobbs's Fourth of July Parade, pictured facing east on the 200 block of West Broadway, is an annual event. It is shown here in 1944. The Trips Hotel is on the left. The Lea

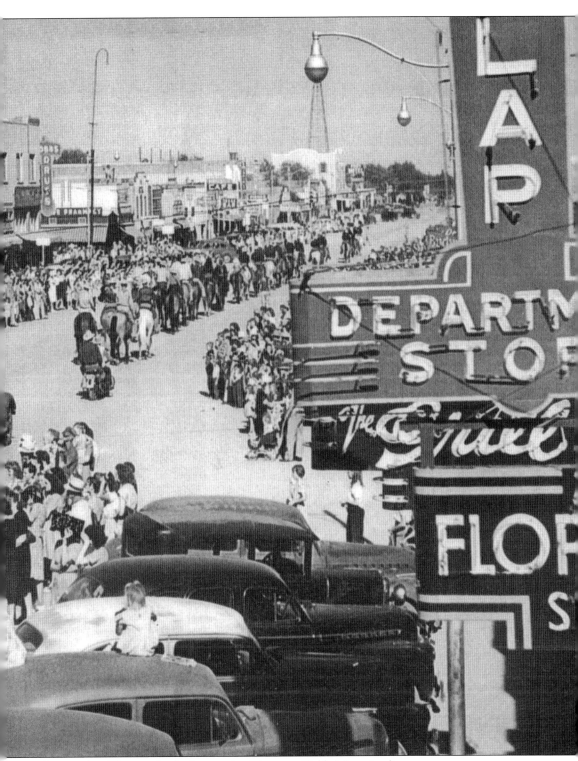
County sheriff's posse leads the parade. (Courtesy *Hobbs News-Sun*.)

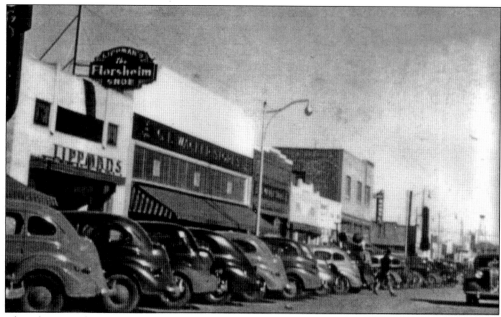

This photograph was taken facing east at the intersection of Broadway and Turner Street in 1940. Among the stores pictured were Lippman's Clothing Store; the G. F. Wacker Variety Store, managed by J. E. "Ed" Vandiver; the JCPenney store; and the Reavis Drug Store. (Courtesy Joe Harvey.)

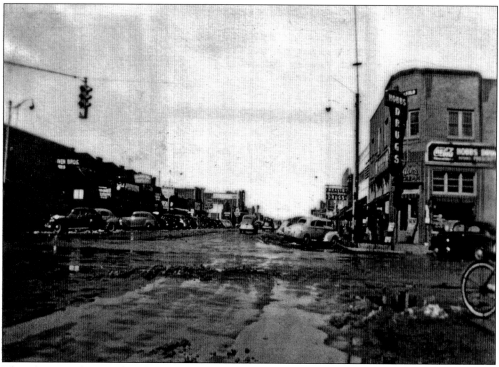

This photograph was taken facing west on West Broadway in 1937. Smokey Motsenbacher's Hobbs Drugs store was on the corner. (Courtesy Joe Harvey.)

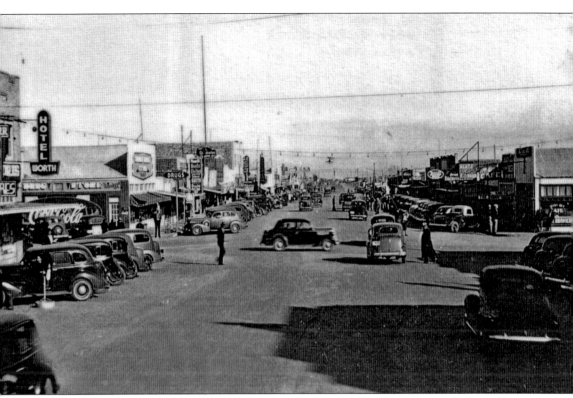

This photograph was taken facing east at the intersection of West Broadway and Shipp Street in 1945. The Furr Food Store is on the left, which was managed by "Chick" Arnold. It was the first store in the Furr food chain. (Courtesy Lois Troutt.)

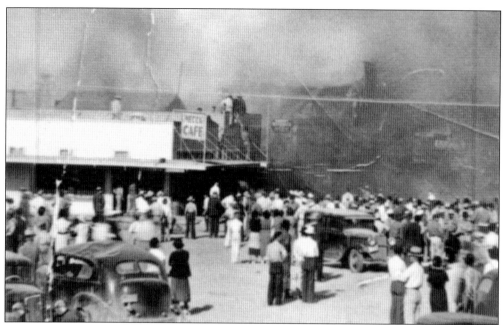

In 1936, the Mecca Café was nearly wiped out by fire on the 100 block of West Carlsbad Street. The café was built by Frank and Ada Capurani in 1929. (Courtesy Lois Troutt.)

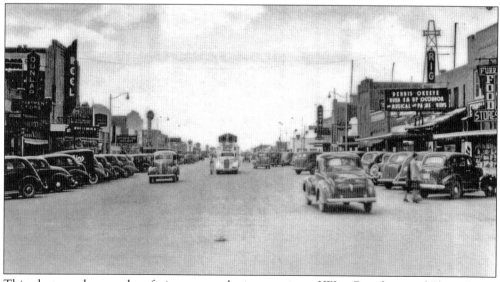

This photograph was taken facing east at the intersection of West Broadway and Shipp Street in 1937. (Courtesy Lois Troutt.)

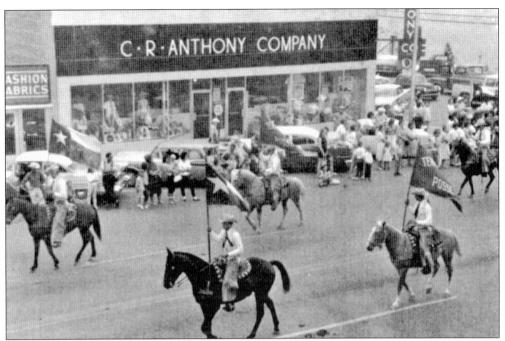

The C. R. Anthony Store was located on West Broadway in 1946. Built in 1937, the clothing store was managed by A. C. Dillon. Pictured in front of the store is the Lea County sheriff's posse. (Courtesy *Hobbs News-Sun*.)

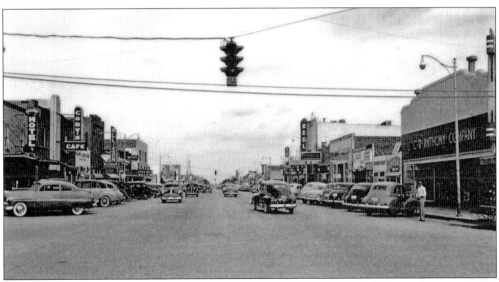

This photograph was taken of the intersection of West Broadway and Linam Street in 1950. (Courtesy *Hobbs News-Sun*.)

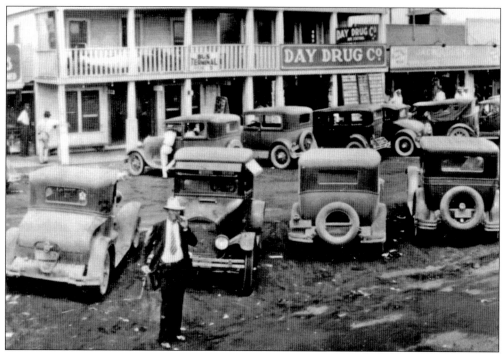
Officer "Pops" Gray, in the foreground, is posed in front of the Jack Coleman store in the 100 block of West Carlsbad Street in 1930. (Courtesy Lois Troutt.)

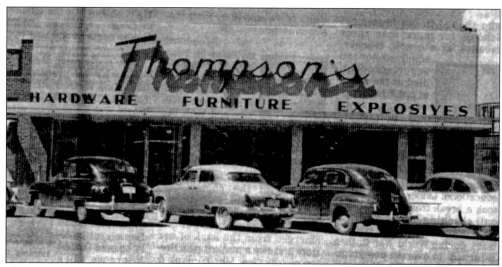
Thompson's Hardware, Furniture, and Explosives was the first permanent, brick structure built in downtown. It was constructed in 1930 at 206 West Broadway. The store was owned and operated by Grady Thompson. (Courtesy Lois Troutt.)

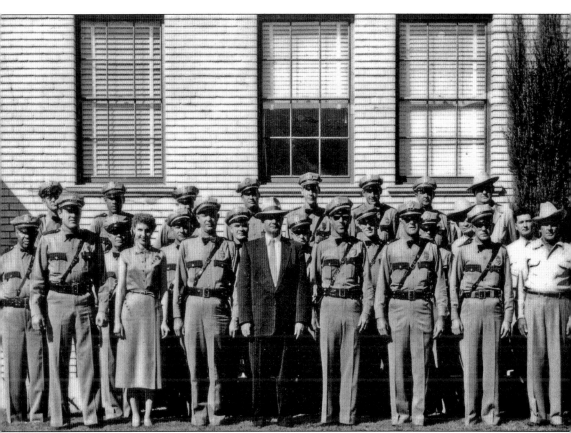

The Hobbs Police Department poses in front of its office building in 1953. From left to right are (first row) Tony Biswell, Jerri Barkley, Homer Phillips, Earl Westfall, L. V. Stevens, Duane Peters, L. V. Rhea, and J. A. Disney; (second row) Horace Weathers, Tokio Vandagriff, Dale Collins, Calvin Whitworth, John Gusha, Frank Anderson, ? Jetton, unidentified, and Pat Thames; (third row) R. B. "Bob" Butler, Jimmy Palmer, Ivan Reed, Gene Jetton, Ennis Jetton, Don Shoults, Floyd Durke, and W. W. Klutting. (Courtesy Hobbs Police Department.)

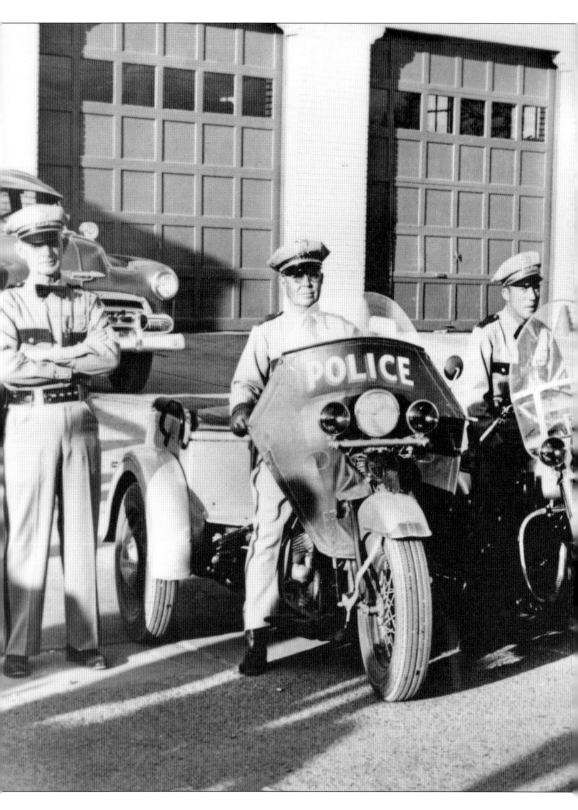

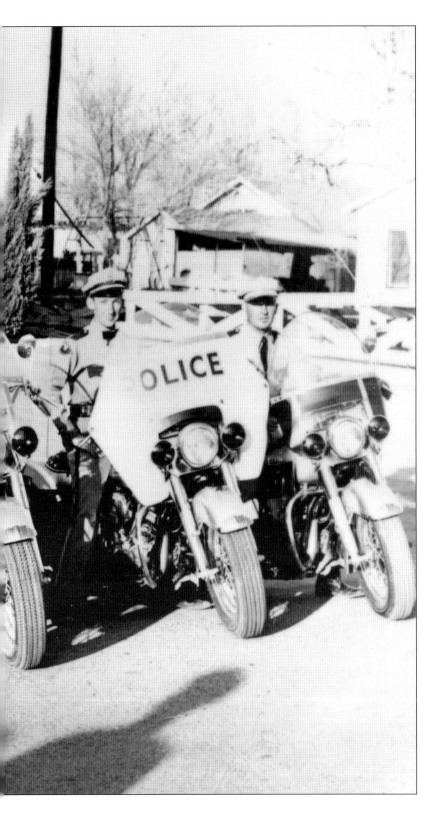

The Hobbs Police Department poses in front of the fire department. From left to right are W. W. Klutting, Tokio Vandagriff, L. V. Rhea, Frank Anderson, and Prince Collins. (Courtesy Hobbs Police Department.)

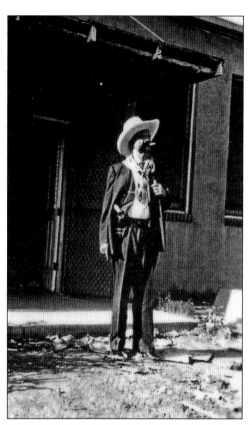

The Hobbs city constable, "Pops" Gray, poses while smoking a cigar and flashing his western revolver in 1930. (Courtesy Jim Rawls.)

The Lea County deputy sheriff was killed on February 25, 1932, during a gunfight with two robbers three miles south of Crossroads. Although mortally wounded, J. M. Clifton managed to draw his weapon and kill both the robbers, John O'Dell and Walter Carlock. Deputy Sherriff Clifton died a few hours later in an airplane as he was being transported to Lubbock for medical care. He was only 27 years old at the time of his death. (Courtesy Lea County Sherriff Department.)

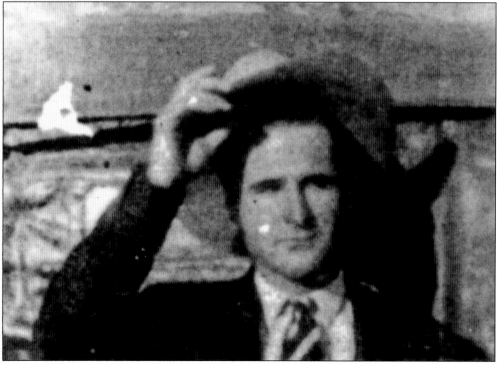

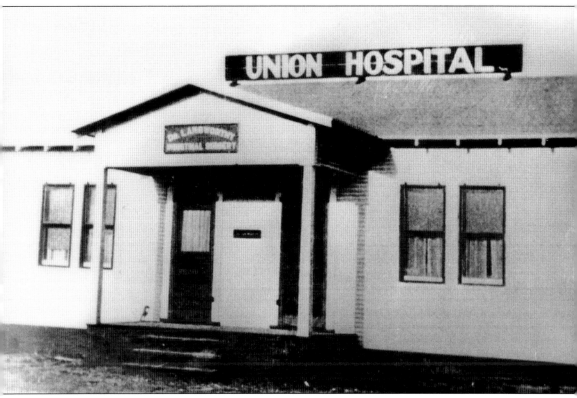

In 1928, the Union Hospital was operated by a Dr. Langworthy for industrial surgery to treat injuries caused by manual labor. Located at 301 East Cain Street, this was the first hospital in Hobbs. (Courtesy Lois Troutt.)

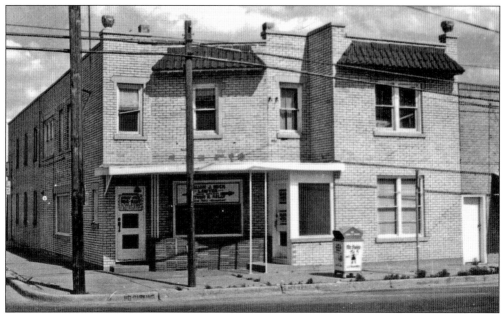

The Medical Arts Clinic was built in March 1931. The clinic's bottom floor had the labs and clinics, while the top floor was equipped with more than 20 hospital beds. The original staff was dentist E. H. Beck and Drs. E. J. Brown, Ben Ard, A. L. Jennings, and C. A. McFadden. The hospital was taken over on April 8, 1932, by Dr. Beck and Dr. Sam Stewart. The name changed to Hobbs General Hospital, which closed in 1934. The building was taken over again by Dr. A. C. Shuler and renamed Shuler Hospital in 1936. It was then sold to Virginia Futch, who advertised in 1938 "having a bed capacity for 6 adults, bassinets for babies, laboratory, x-ray, and completely-equipped operating room." In 1941, it was sold to Dr. Allen P. Terrell, and the name changed to Terrell Hospital. Terrell operated it until his death in 1947. (Courtesy Joe Harvey.)

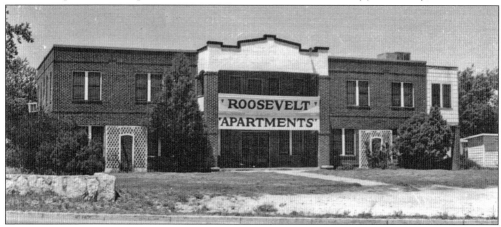

The second hospital in Hobbs was built by John J. Harden. The first doctors in Hobbs were Dr. George McClean and Dr. C. J. Conner in 1930. The construction took place in 1930, but the hospital closed on March 1, 1933, when the Great Depression drove the doctors from Hobbs. The hospital was converted first into the Roosevelt Tavern, which opened on April 4, 1934, but closed three months later because of an illegal liquor license. Soon thereafter, the tavern was remodeled into the Roosevelt Apartments. (Note the caliche rock fence, built by stonemason "Duke" Ives. He built these fences all over Hobbs in those days.) (Courtesy Lois Troutt.)

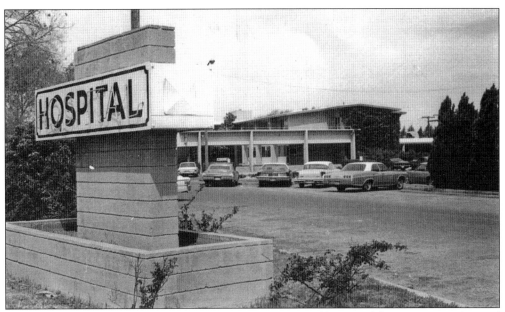

The Lea County General Hospital was built in 1947 as the Hobbs unit of the Lea County General Hospital System. Currently, the hospital is leased to Evangelical Lutheran Health Care. (Courtesy Lois Troutt.)

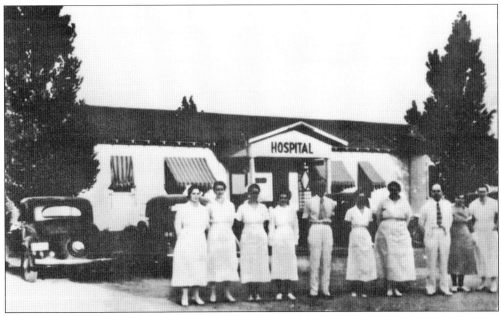

Posed outside of Dr. Coy S. Stone's hospital in the 300 block of East Cabin Street is the staff five years after the hospital was built. From left to right are Ruby Collins, Elizabeth Davis, Zena McCasland, Wilheima Marshall, H. B. Lloyd, Josey Sullivan, Vivian Pippin, Dr. Coy Smith Stone, Mattie Williams, and Leona Lloyd. The hospital was built in 1930 by the Continental Oil Company. (Courtesy Lois Troutt.)

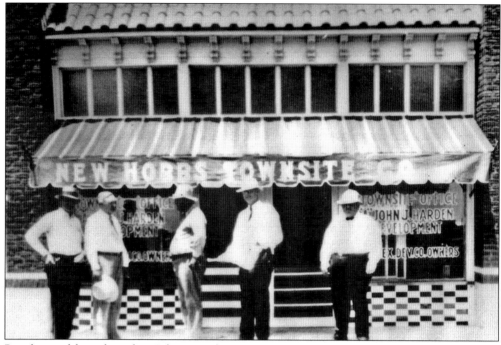

Posed second from the right is John J. Harden in 1930. Harden built the Harden Hotel for $200,000. The Mex-Tex Townsite subdivided Main Street in New Hobbs. (Courtesy Ed Seabourne.)

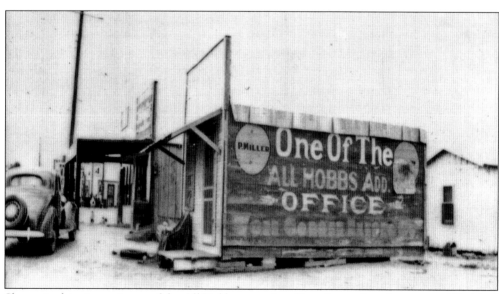

Shown in this picture is one of the All Hobbs town site offices, located on the corner of Carlsbad and Dal Paso Streets, in 1935. The town site office for the All Hobbs subdivision was owned by Ed and Lola McLaughlin, Paul and Kay Miller, and J. H. and Mollie Edwards. The town site was dedicated on February 18, 1930, and was bounded by East Marland, South Dal Paso, East Snyder, and South Jefferson Streets. (Courtesy Ed Seabourne.)

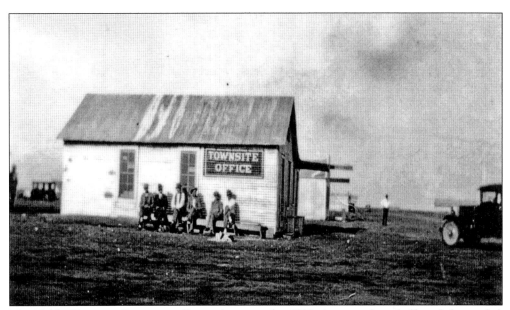

The Hobbs Townsite Company office is shown in this 1929 photograph with (from left to right) shareholders J. J. Carson, A. G. Trout, J. R. Harris, K. F. Albright, A. W. Board, and unidentified. (Courtesy Lois Troutt.)

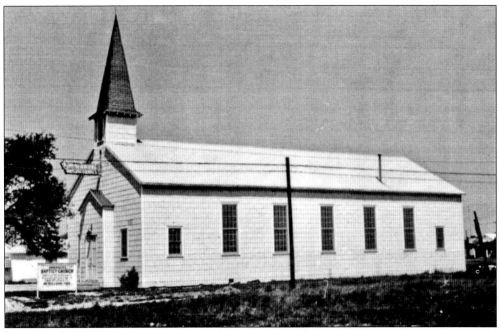

The Immanuel Baptist Church was one of the chapels at the Hobbs Army Air Base in 1942 and is still in use today. (Courtesy Ed Seabourne.)

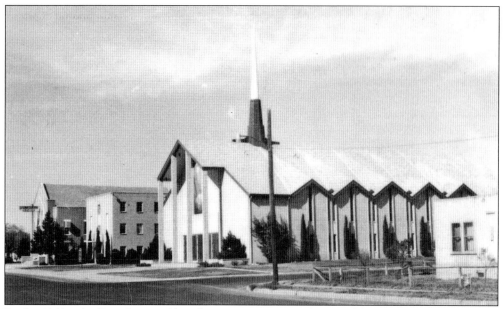
In the 1960s, the First Baptist Church sanctuary was a welcome addition to Hobbs. (Courtesy First Baptist Church.)

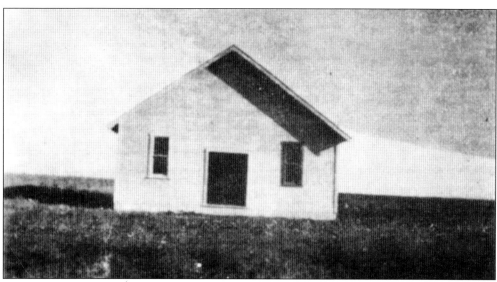
This photograph shows the First Baptist Church, which was constructed in 1929 at 300 East Cain Street on the same site as the present First Baptist Church building. The two lots for the building were donated by the Hobbs Townsite Company. (Courtesy Lois Troutt.)

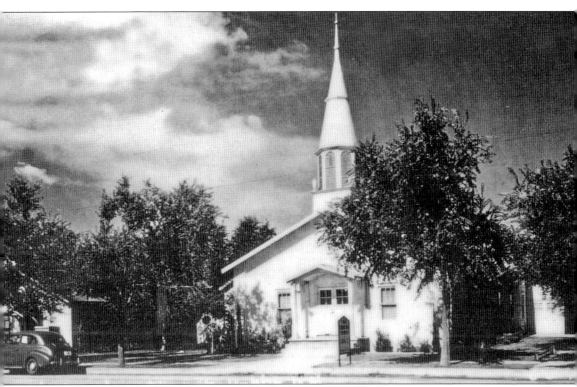
The First Christian Church in Hobbs was built on Turner Street in 1940. (Courtesy Lois Troutt.)

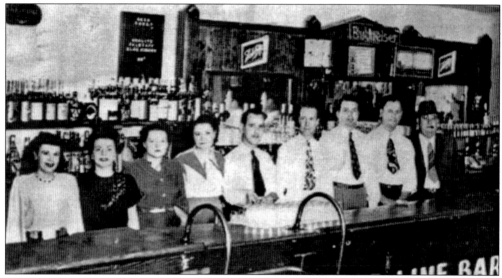
Al's State Line Bar and dance hall was located on the south side of the Seminole Highway across the highway from Club Morrice. (Courtesy Ed Seabourne.)

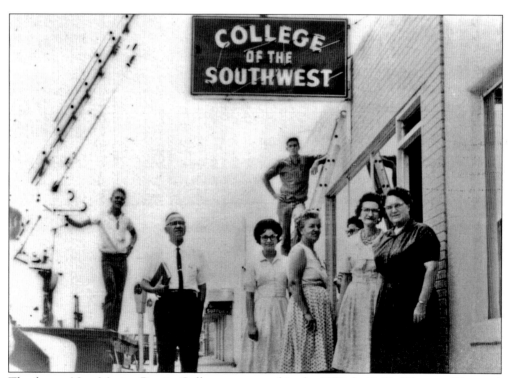
The former New Mexico Baptist College was started in the 1950s by B. C. (Bloomer Clarence) Evans, second from the left, Bible in hand. The Baptist College is in the 200 block of North Shipp Street. (Courtesy Lois Troutt.)

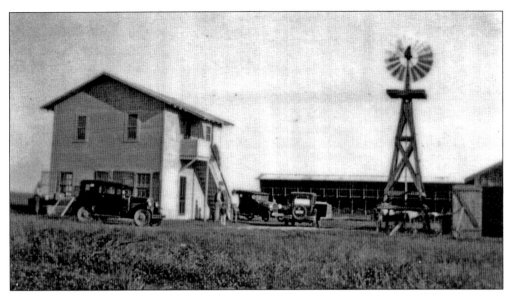
The Wooldridge Lumber Yard was located on 500 East Dunham Street in 1928. (Courtesy Lois Troutt.)

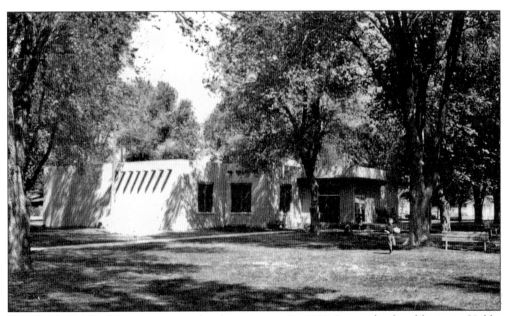
The Hobbs Public Library was completed on August 21, 1939. It was the first library in Hobbs and was a project of the Hobbs Civic Club. The Clinton Park land site was donated by Jennie Clinton. (Courtesy Lois Troutt.)

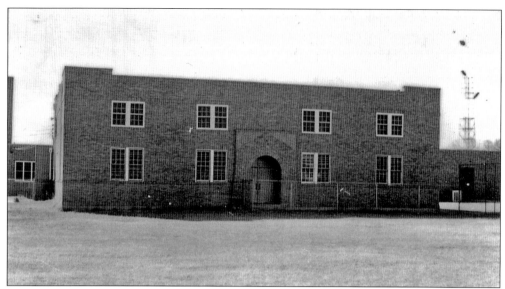

The Will Rogers Gym was located at 600 North Dalmont and was built in 1935. The high school played its games there through 1938. (Courtesy Hobbs Municipal Schools.)

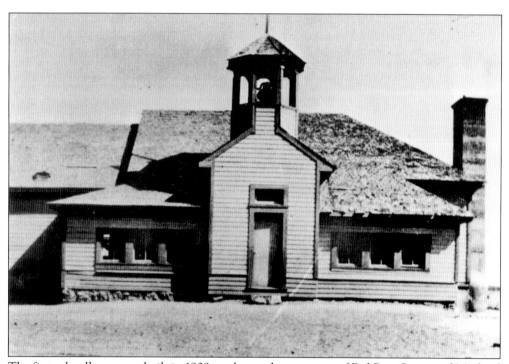

The first schoolhouse was built in 1909 on the southeast corner of Dal Paso Street and Marland Boulevard. It was a 14-by-16-foot frame structure. The first paid teacher was Cornelius Land. The second schoolhouse built in Hobbs, shown in this photograph, was constructed by Ernest Byers in 1915 and was located on the northeast corner of the same intersection. The first classes were held in the basement while the building was under construction. The Eden schoolhouse was moved to town and was attached to the building pictured here. (Courtesy Thelma Linam.)

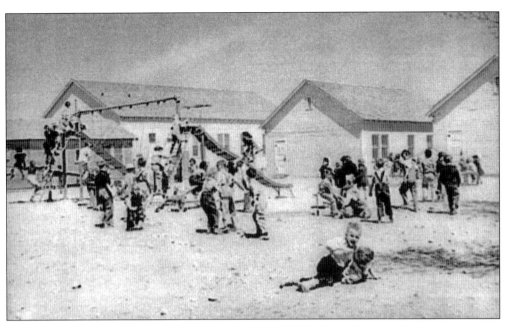

The South Hobbs Elementary School was located at 501 West Gypsy Street in 1937, which is now the Edison School. (Courtesy Hobbs Public Schools.)

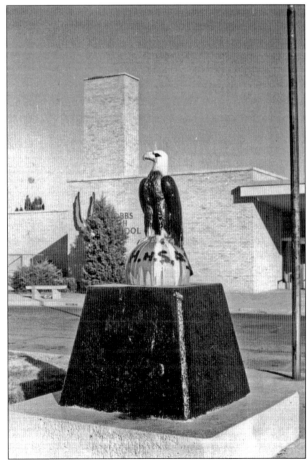

This statue was stolen from an implement dealer in Lovington by Hobbs High School students in 1973. Almost every year the statue must be repainted after Lovington students decorate it with their school colors. (Courtesy Hobbs Public Schools.)

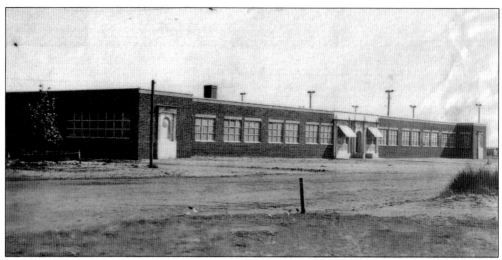

The Hobbs High School was built in 1935 for $80,000 and was located at 300 North Houston Street. This is the present location of the Houston Junior High School. The combination of the gym and auditorium was added on the next year. The football field was on the south end of the building. (Courtesy Hobbs Fire Department.)

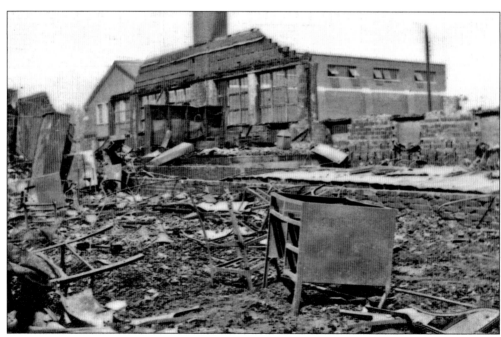

Burned rubble was all that was left after the April 6, 1943, fire destroyed Hobbs High School. The gym in the background was the only part of the school left untouched by the fire. (Courtesy Hobbs Fire Department.)

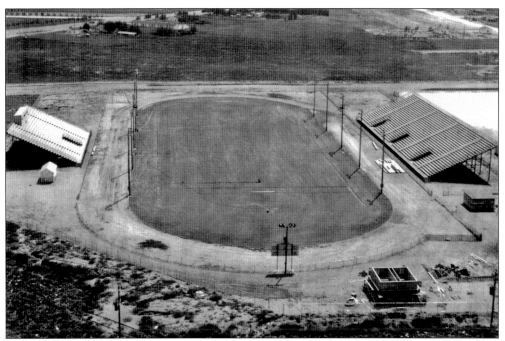
The Watson Stadium, built in 1950, was named for Finn Watson, who was the longtime chairman of the Hobbs Municipal School Board. (Courtesy Hobbs Public Schools.)

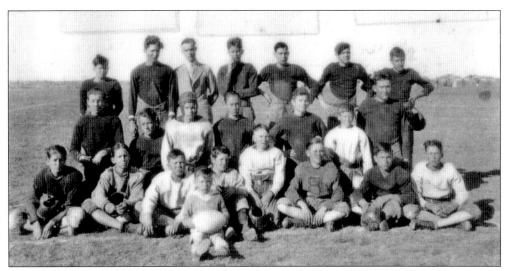
This photograph shows the Hobbs High School football team in 1932–1933. The playing field was located in the 1000 block of North Shipp Street. From left to right are (first row) Wilford Weske, W. T. Coleman, Earl Burleson, Raymond Stephens, Birch Bostic, Hamilton Walker, Gaviel Yates, and Travis Thompson; (second row) Jack Roberts, Boyce Appleton, Van Baker, Denvil Tucker, Byron Fletcher, "Red" Fletcher, and Aubrey Childers; (third row) Hamilton Walker, W. L. Dunham, coach John Witt (in the suit), Andrew Boroughs, James Caylor, R. E. Wells, and Faye Baker. Barney Hynds, the football mascot, is sitting with the game ball in front of the team. (Courtesy Hobbs Public Schools.)

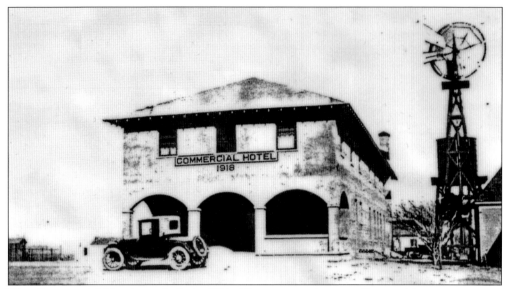

The Commercial Hotel was built in 1918. The construction was financed by a corporation whose members included J. D. Graham, M. E. Sewalt, Seth Alston, and G. M. McGonagil. The Commercial Hotel was later named the Plaza. In 2007, the Plaza was purchased and became the Lea County Museum, which is now managed by Jim Harris. (Courtesy *Lovington Leader*.)

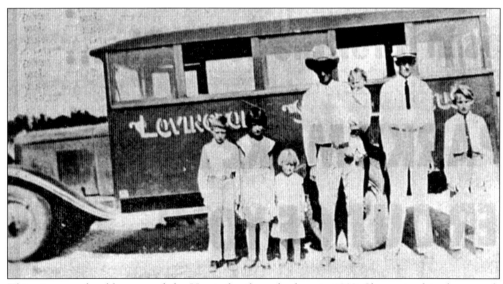

This vintage school bus served the Harris family and others in 1932. Shown in this photograph (from left to right) are Paul Harris, Lily Mae Harris, Burl Harris, Robert Harris (holding Virginia Lee Harris), and two unidentified. (Courtesy Jim Harris.)

Four

BOOMTOWNS, THE GREAT DEPRESSION, AND WORLD WAR II

In the early days of 1927, "Boom at Hobbs" was the headline news that transformed an area where the only thing one could see in any direction was one windmill, two trees, a small general-merchandise store building, and a little ranch house. But this tranquil scene was about to change, almost overnight, as oil was discovered. But of course, the world had other plans, and the Great Depression hit.

When the Great Depression first impacted the United States, it would be nearly a year before it began to really affect Hobbs. It took that long for the "boom" of the previous three years to wind down. But when oil started selling for 10¢ a barrel, Hobbs slowed down in a hurry. A few folks elected to stay and just try to "tough it out." People here had just begun to move out of tents, cardboard shacks, and two or three "shotgun" houses. When the oil field almost completely shut down, they had to leave and try to find work elsewhere. But the hits kept coming as America re-entered the world's second war.

In 1940, the storm clouds of World War II continued to gather, and it became evident the United States could not remain neutral much longer. The City of Hobbs began a campaign to become a part of the spirited competition for the establishment of an army air base. On April 7, 1942, it was announced that an Army Air Corps flight training base would be located in the small town.

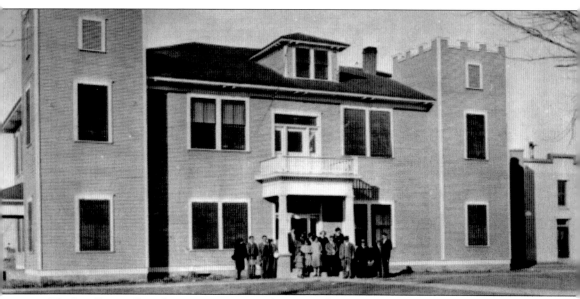

The Lea County Courthouse was constructed in 1918. The courthouse is in Lovington, facing south. (Courtesy Jim Harris.)

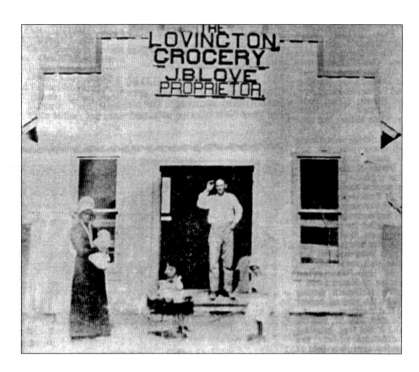

Lovington's first general-merchandise store was owned by Jim B. Love and his wife. It opened on May 7, 1908. (Courtesy Wade Shipley.)

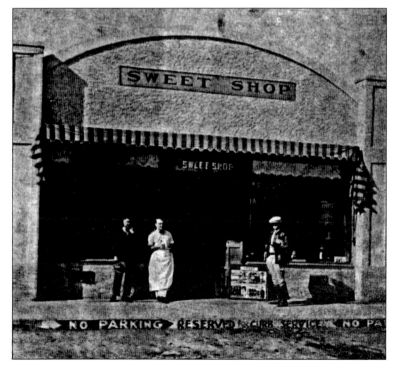

The Sweet Shop in Lovington was a gathering place for the younger group in the early days. Grace Beauchamp, formerly Grace Love, was a "soda jerker" here before she met the young circuit-riding preacher W. M. Beauchamp, who is now the district clerk. (Courtesy Wade Shipley.)

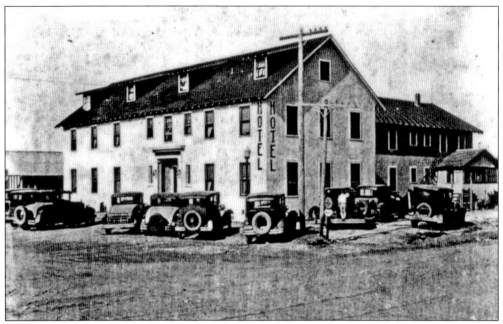

The old Main Hotel was razed in 1964. It was built in the 1930s at the corner of South Main Street and the Artesia Highway. It was operated for many years by Effie Fairweather Chamberlain, who still resides in Lovington. The name "Fair-weather Hotel" can be seen over the door. (Courtesy Wade Shipley.)

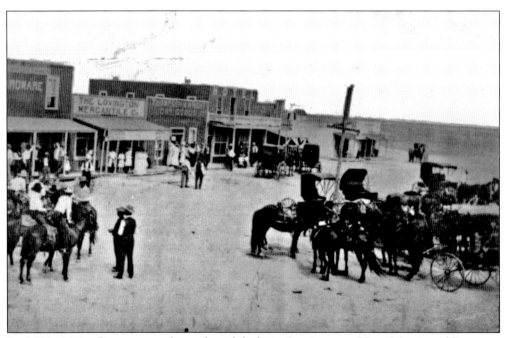

In 1911, Main Street was the cultural hub in Lovington, New Mexico. (Courtesy Lea County Museum.)

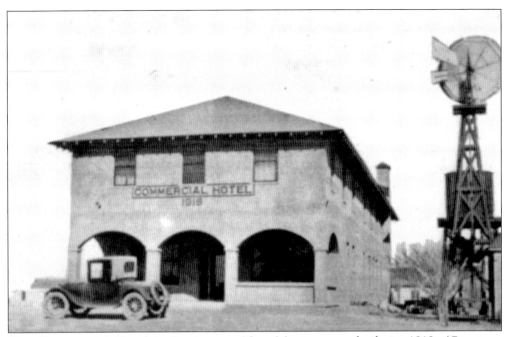
The Commercial Hotel in Lovington, New Mexico, was built in 1918. (Courtesy Lea County Museum.)

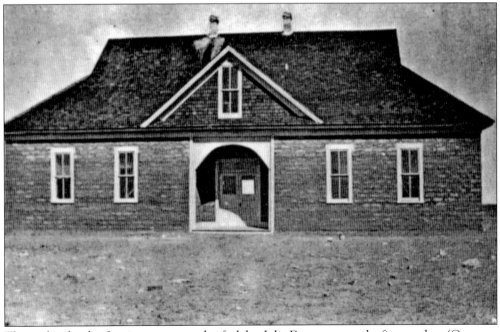
This early school in Lovington was made of adobe. Julia Dunaway was the first teacher. (Courtesy Ernest Byers.)

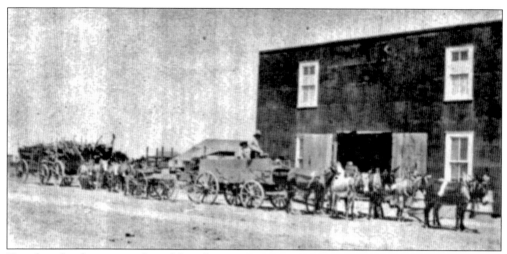

Traveling freighters move down Main Street in Lovington in 1911. Among the businesses on this street were the feed store and the stable. (Courtesy Lea County Museum.)

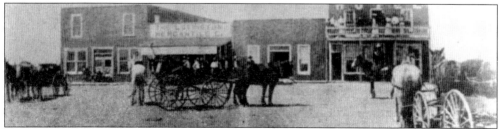

Local shops, including the post office and the doctor's office, provided their services in these buildings in Lovington, New Mexico, in 1910. (Courtesy Ernest Byers.)

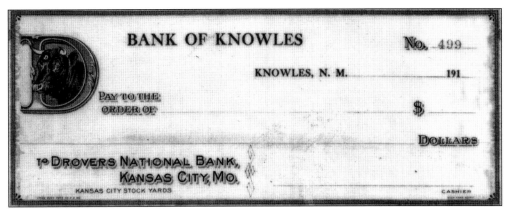

The Bank of Knowles was a branch of the Drovers National Bank in Kansas City, Missouri, in the 1910s. (Courtesy Knowles Fire Department.)

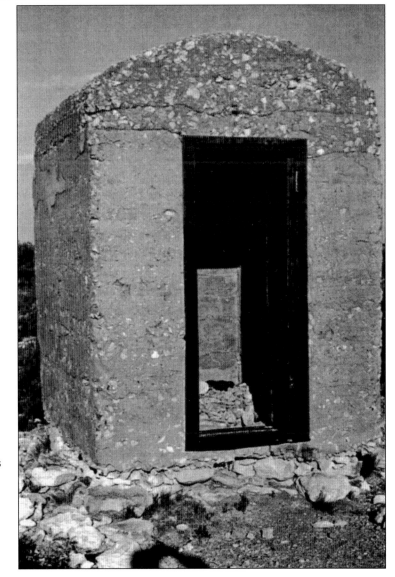

This bank vault of the Bank of Knowles in Lovington (right) was built in 1910, although the photograph was taken in 1975. (Courtesy Knowles Fire Department.)

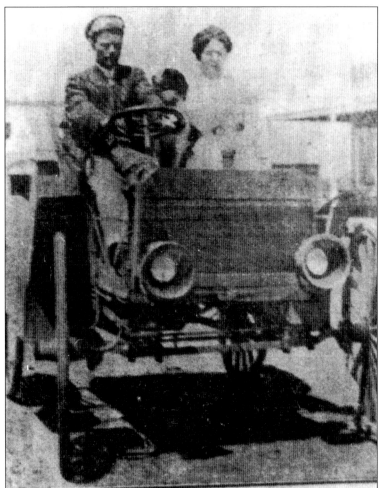

Dr. H. W. Sellers drives his new automobile in Knowles, New Mexico, in 1910. (Courtesy Knowles Fire Department.)

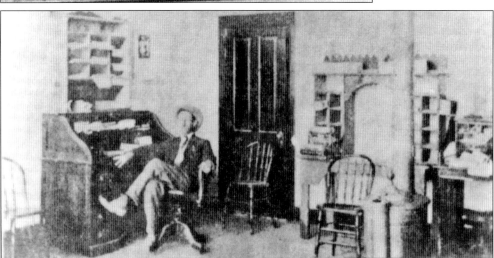

Pictured here is the office of Jesse C. Reeves, who was also the former U.S. court commissioner in 1910. (Courtesy Knowles Fire Department.)

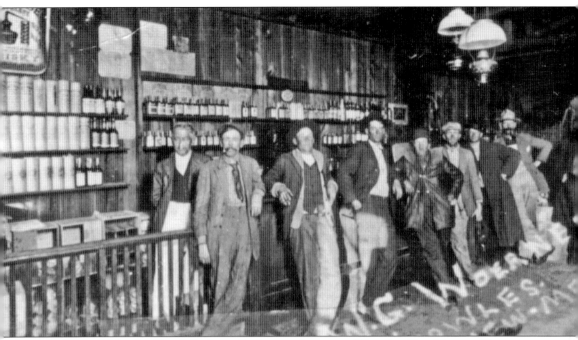
Pictured in 1906 is the "Stock Exchange" saloon in the town of Knowles, New Mexico. (Courtesy Wade Shipley.)

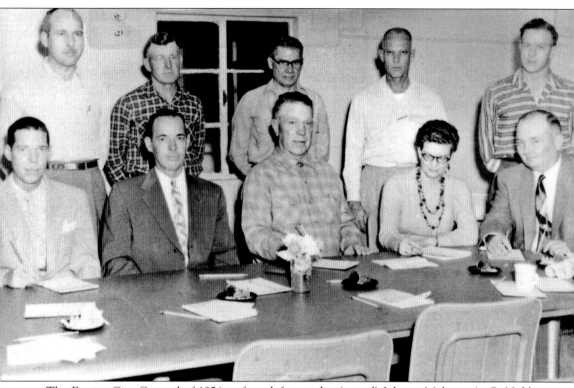

The Eunice City Council of 1954 is, from left to right, (seated) Johnny Malone, A. G. Noble, Mayor Pete Stevens, city clerk Sylvia Houston, and Truman Turner; (standing) Mayor Pro Tem Max A. Clampitt, W. A. Davis, C. H. "Hicks" Martin, Oliver Wildman, and Donald Gladden. Not shown is city attorney Bill Heck. (Courtesy Max Clampitt.)

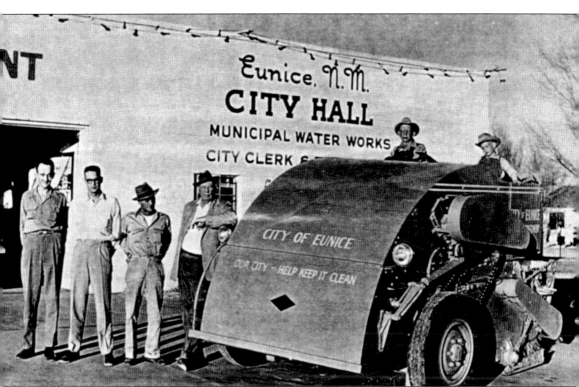

In front of the Eunice, New Mexico, City Hall (which also housed the Municipal Water Works and city clerk office) are, from left to right, city clerk Glenn Schrader, city councilman T. D. "Dale" Skelton, "Buck" Nolen, and Mayor Early Fletcher; on top of the street sweeper is "Dad" Ray and his grandson in 1952. (Courtesy City of Eunice, New Mexico, Eunice Public Library.)

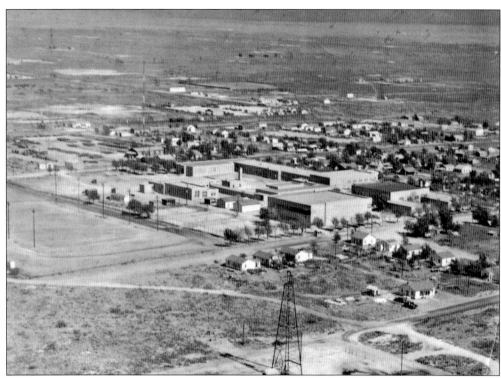

The Eunice High School Football field, shown in 1949, provided great entertainment for residents on Friday nights. (Courtesy Eunice Public Schools, Eunice Public Library.)

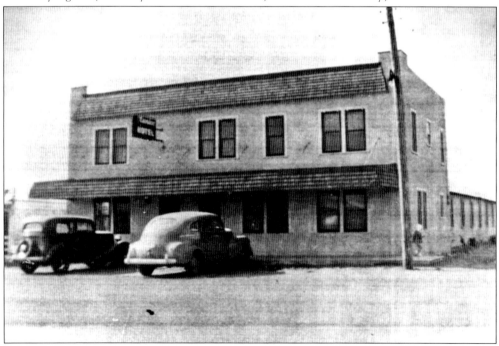

The Eunice Hotel was built on Main Street and Avenue I. The back part was moved from Shafter Lake in Texas. This photograph was taken in 1949. (Courtesy *Eunice Starr*.)

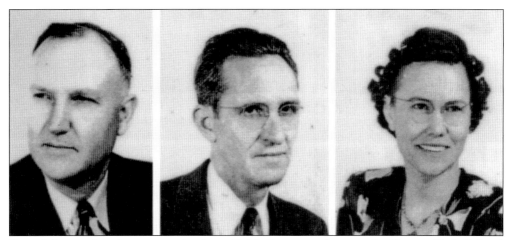

From left to right, these portraits show C. H. Conway, who was the Eunice High School superintendent from 1937 to 1962; J. W. Caton, the high school principal from 1937 to 1962 who went on to become the superintendent from 1962 to 1968; and Mettie Jordan, who was the Lea County superintendant from 1934 to 1936. Jordan was also a teacher in 1925 and the grade school principal from 1937 to 1969. (Courtesy Eunice, New Mexico, Public Schools.)

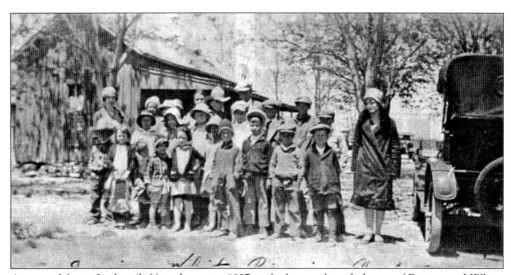

A young Mettie Jordan (left) is shown in 1927 with the combined classes of Eunice and White Schools. The occasion was a spring picnic held at the 84 Ranch. The woman on the right was Ora May Medlin, teacher at the White School. (Courtesy Eunice, New Mexico, Public Schools.)

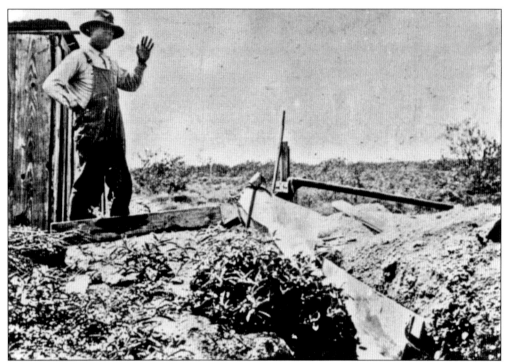
Pleasant Valley is shown in 1926 as S. P. Jordan, Mettie's father, ran irrigation. (Courtesy Max Clampitt.)

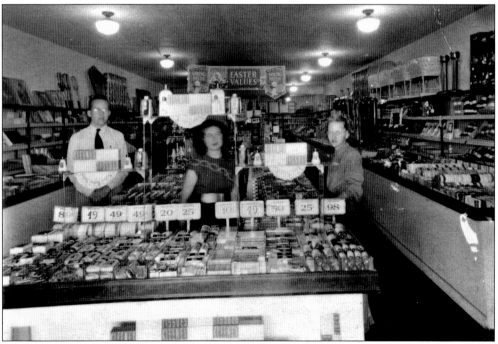
Pictured is the G. F. Wacker Store in Eunice, New Mexico, in 1949. From left to right are store manager Max A. Clampitt, Annie Merle Henderson, and Rose Melva Sowell. (Courtesy Max Clampitt.)

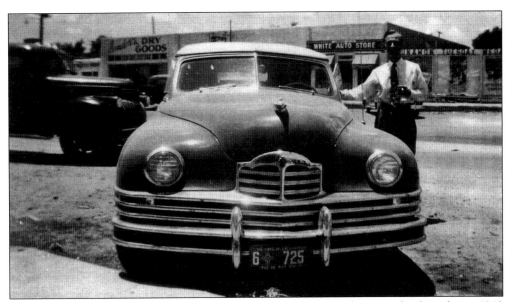

In front of the White Auto Store, Dr. William Bruner is pictured next to his brand-new 1948 Ford Packard convertible in Eunice, New Mexico. (Courtesy Max Clampitt.)

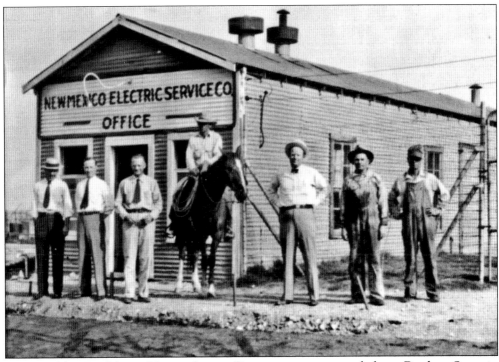

In front of the New Mexico Electric Service Company are company clerks on Dunham Street in the 1930s. (Courtesy New Mexico Electric Service Company.)

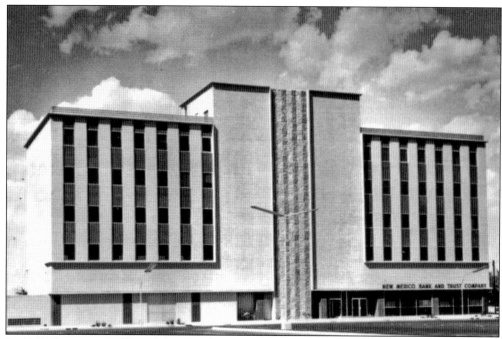

In 1961, the general office of the Broadmoor Shopping Center provided wonderful services for the community. (Courtesy New Mexico Electric Service Company.)

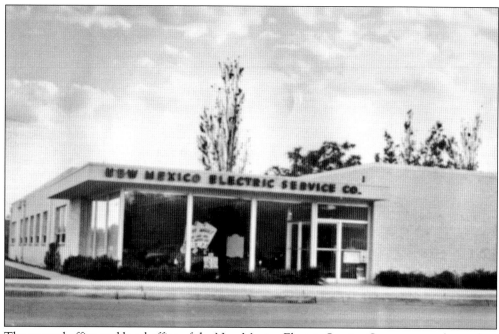

The general office and local office of the New Mexico Electric Service Company was located on East Dunham Street in 1961. It was reconstructed in 1953 at the same location. (Courtesy New Mexico Electric Service Company.)

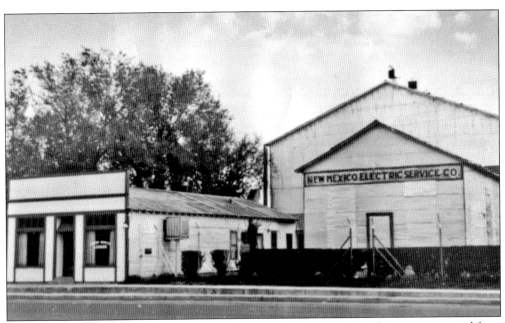

The general office and local office of the New Mexico Electric Service Company operated from 1936 to 1953 at 221 East Dunham Street. (Courtesy New Mexico Electric Service Company.)

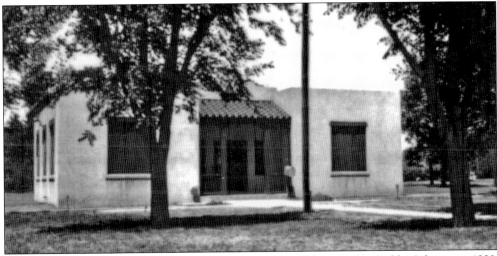

A wealth of knowledge and research material was available at Hobbs Public Library in 1939. (Courtesy Hobbs City Library.)

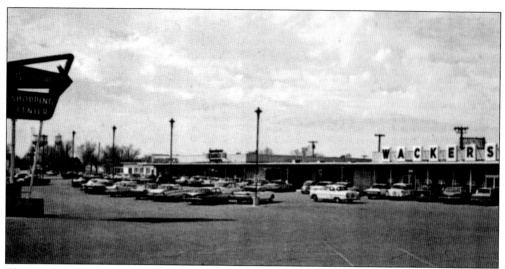

The Wackers Store was one of many that drew in Hobbs's citizens to the Broadmoor Shopping Center located on North Turner and Sanger Streets in 1960. (Courtesy Joe Harvey.)

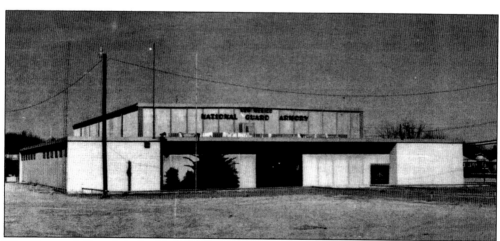

The National Guard Armory is currently known as the John J. Fletcher Center. The city traded land on the old air base for this building. The photograph was taken in 1974. (Courtesy Joe Harvey.)

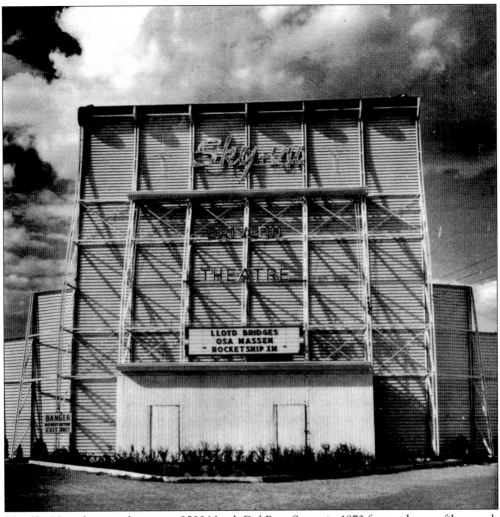
The Sky View drive-in theater on 2500 North Dal Paso Street in 1973 featured many films, such as the Lloyd Bridges and Osa Massen film *Rocketship X-M*. (Courtesy Joe Harvey.)

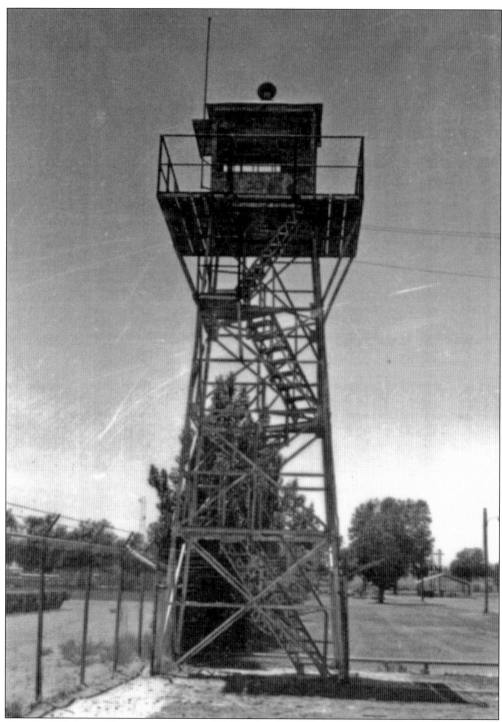
The Civil Defense Observation Tower in Hobbs City Park was built in the 1950s and was manned by a group of volunteers. This tower was built to watch for possible air attacks from Russian bombers during the cold war era. This photograph was taken in 1973. (Courtesy Joe Harvey.)

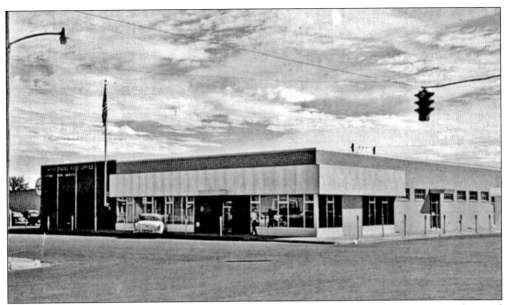

The Hobbs City Post Office was located on the corner of Shipp and Taylor Streets and served the city from 1963 to 1998. Max A. Clampitt was one of the many employees who worked for the postal service during that time; he worked there for 28 years. (Courtesy Max Clampitt.)

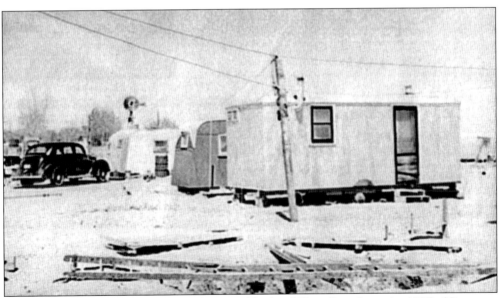

The trailer park was located in the 400 block of East Broadway in 1935. (Courtesy Ed Seabourne.)

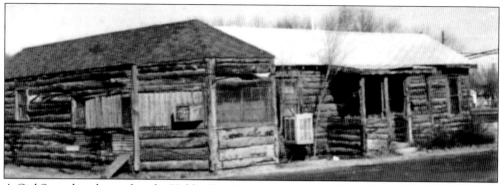

A Girl Scout hut, located in the Hobbs City Park, was condemned in 1974 and razed after having been in service for more than 20 years. (Courtesy City of Hobbs, Park Department.)

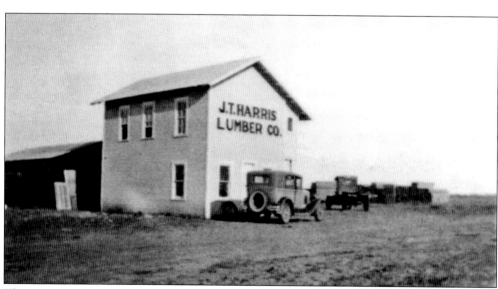

The J. T. Harris Lumber Company provided lumber for Hobbs in 1929 and was in business for many years at 207 North Shipp Street. (Courtesy Lois Troutt.)

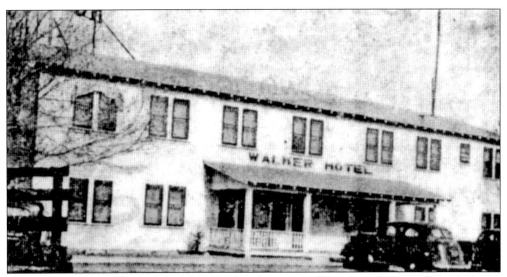

An early photograph shows the Walker Hotel at the corner of East Cain Street and North Fowler Street and west of Dr. Coy S. Stone's hospital. The hotel provided the latest luxuries Hobbs had to offer its visitors. (Courtesy Lois Troutt.)

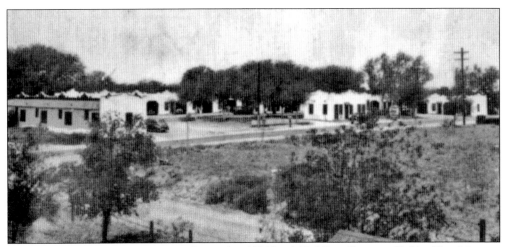

The Hillcrest apartment courts were located at 409 North Dal Paso Street in Hobbs, New Mexico. (Courtesy Lois Troutt.)

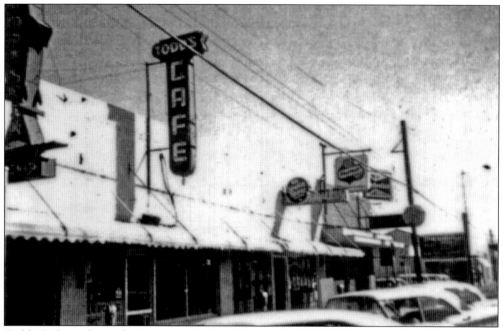

Todd's Café was located at 107 East Dunham Street in 1970 in Hobbs. It served as a hiring center for local job hunters. (Courtesy Joe Harvey.)

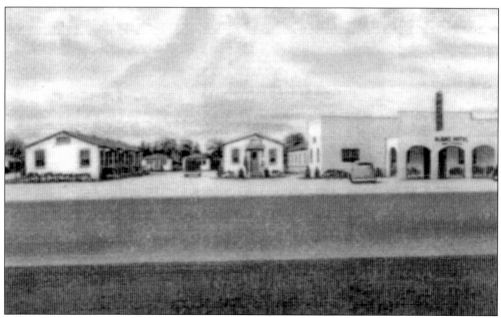

The Plains Hotel and Courts, located on Highways 180 and 62 in Hobbs, New Mexico, provided a lovely stay for weary travelers and tourists. (Courtesy Joe Harvey.)

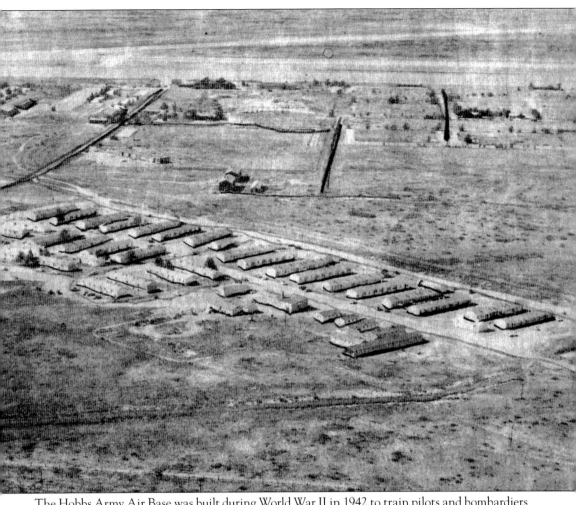

The Hobbs Army Air Base was built during World War II in 1942 to train pilots and bombardiers for B-17 Flying Fortress bombers. (Courtesy City of Hobbs, Engineering Department.)

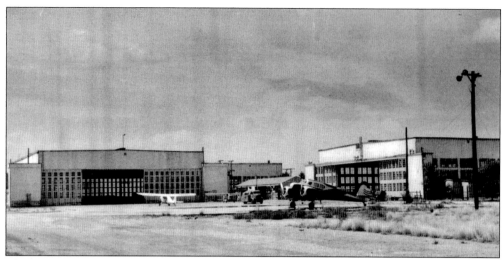
The B-17 hangar moved to the Lea County Airport for Confederate Air Force (CAF) use in the 1940s. Note the Piper Cub and Twin Beechcraft aircrafts. (Courtesy City of Hobbs, Engineering Department.)

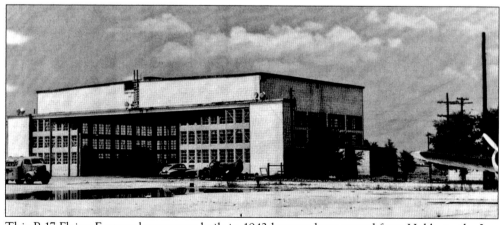
This B-17 Flying Fortress hangar was built in 1943 but was later moved from Hobbs to the Lea County Airport for CAF use. (Courtesy City of Hobbs, Engineering Department.)

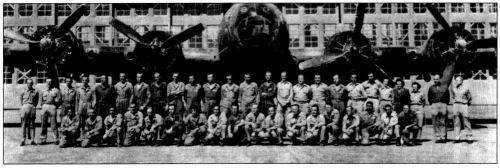

The administrative personnel of the 959th 8th Squadron at the Hobbs Army Air Field posed for this photograph in the 1940s. (Courtesy City of Hobbs, Engineering Department.)

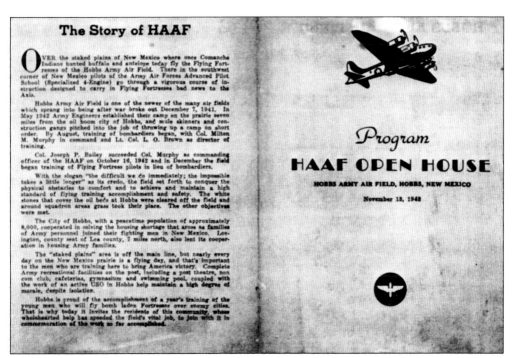

The Hobbs Army Air Field (HAAF) was one of the newer of the many air fields that sprang into being after war broke out on December 7, 1941. Hobbs is proud of the accomplishment of a year's training of the young men who flew bomb-laden Flying Fortresses over enemy cities during World War II. (Courtesy City of Hobbs, Engineering Department.)

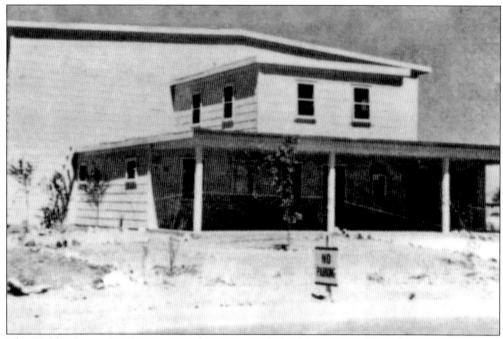
The Hobbs Army Air Base movie theater provided soldiers a much-needed escape in 1943. (Courtesy City of Hobbs, Engineering Department.)

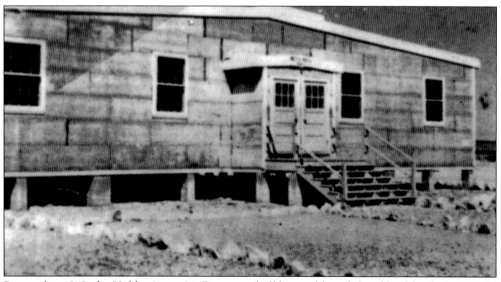
Pictured in 1943, the Hobbs Army Air Base mess hall kept soldiers fed and healthy during World War II. (Courtesy City of Hobbs, Engineering Department.)

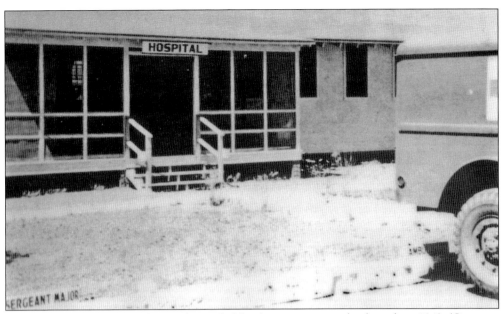
The Hobbs Army Air Base hospital provided for the necessary medical needs in 1943. (Courtesy City of Hobbs, Engineering Department.)

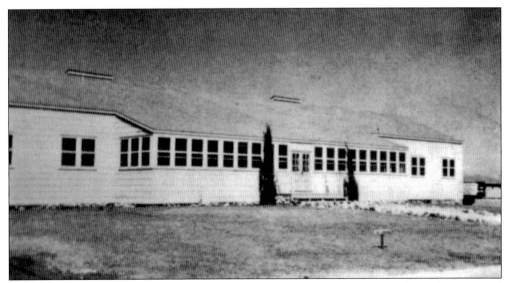
Pictured in 1943, the Hobbs Army Air Base's commissioned officers' club was built during World War II. (Courtesy City of Hobbs, Engineering Department.)

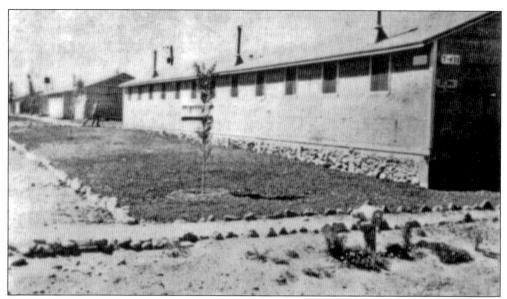
The Hobbs Army Air Base squadron office and barracks housed soldiers in 1943. (Courtesy City of Hobbs, Engineering Department.)

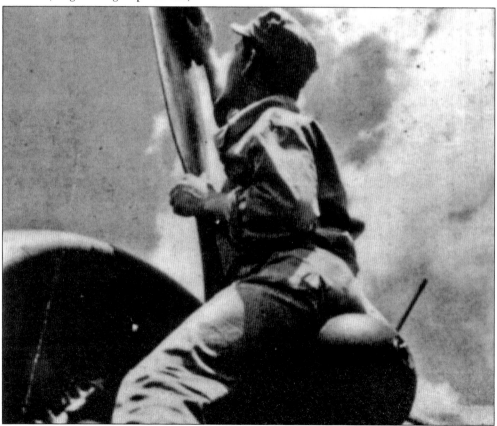
A Hobbs Army Air Base ground crewman cleans a propeller of one of the many airplanes in the hangar in 1943. (Courtesy City of Hobbs, Engineering Department.)

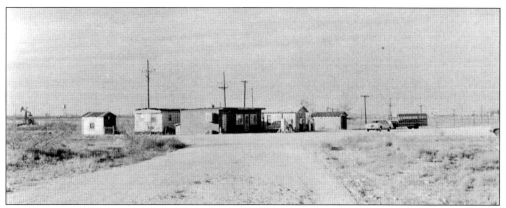
In 1974, Buckeye, New Mexico, was located eight miles south of Lovington, New Mexico. (Courtesy Naomi Hogue.)

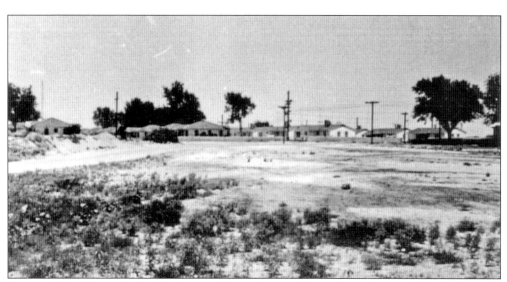
Bennett, New Mexico's school and post office are located five miles southwest of Jal. Also located here are the El Paso Natural Gas Company and several houses for its employees. (Courtesy Naomi Hogue.)

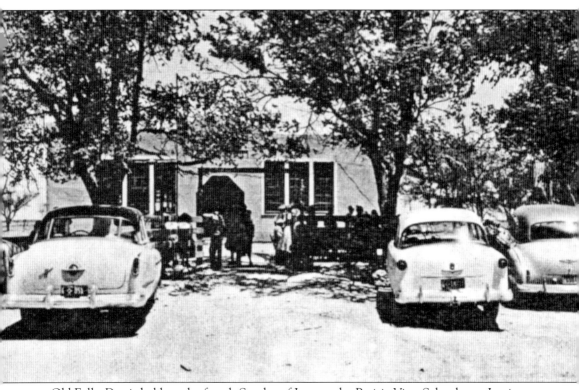
Old Folks Day is held on the fourth Sunday of June at the Prairie View School near Lovington. Old Folks Day was organized to honor the old people of the community. People come from all over the county to attend this reunion every year. (Courtesy Naomi Hogue.)

Five

Economic Development

Demographic developmental studies in Hobbs and Lea County forecasted the new economy with two entities and updated the census by developing new population estimates and projections, which reflect the changes that have taken place since the last census in the year 2000.

Some of the findings revealed that the population of Lea County, previously projected to slowly decline to less than 50,000 by the year 2030, is now expected to exceed 73,000 in that year. That figure reflects an influx of economic migrants attracted to this area by high oil prices and the opening up of job opportunities in other industries, such as the National Enrichment Facility currently under construction 18 miles south of Hobbs. Five miles east of Eunice, the influx of economic migrants, who are predominantly in their peak reproductive and productive years, will have a continued residual effect on the population of Hobbs and Lea County during the next 20 years.

While the surge of oil and gas prices has accounted for a substantial proportion of the new jobs and income growth in this area during the past few years, there is some basis for optimism that the economy will continue to expand as a result of increased diversification of the economy. First, global energy markets are such today that the price of oil is likely to remain high for the foreseeable future. These high prices should be conducive to continued exploration, drilling, and oil well enhancement activities in the proven rich deposits of the Permian Basin. Second, there are new sources of job creation; it is significant that the region has a new future in energy, one based less on fossil fuel and more on energy alternatives, particularly nuclear. There are other developments, including the construction of a 550-megawatt combined-cycle generating plant about six miles west of Hobbs.

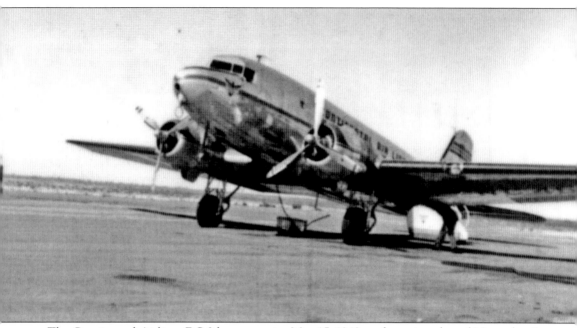

The Continental Airlines DC-3 began service May 15, 1940, and continued until November 5, 1963. Continental Airlines was replaced by Trans-Texas Airlines. The aircraft is parked in front of the terminal at the Lea County Airport. (Courtesy Max Clampitt.)

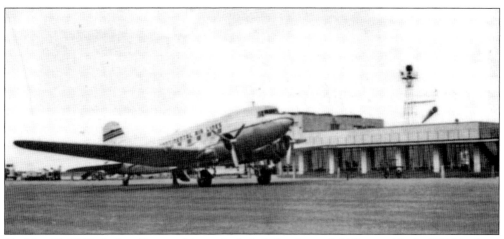

On May 15, 1948, the Lea County Airport included Continental Airlines, with the DC-3 in front of the terminal building. (Courtesy Max Clampitt.)

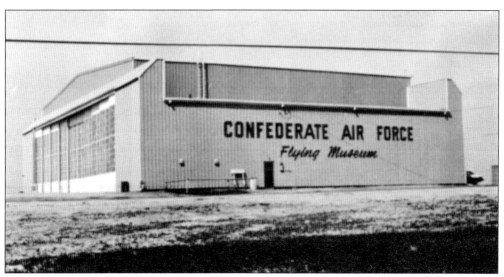

This B-17 hangar was built in 1942 at the Hobbs Army Air Base. The hangar was moved across the county to the municipal airport. (Courtesy Max Clampitt.)

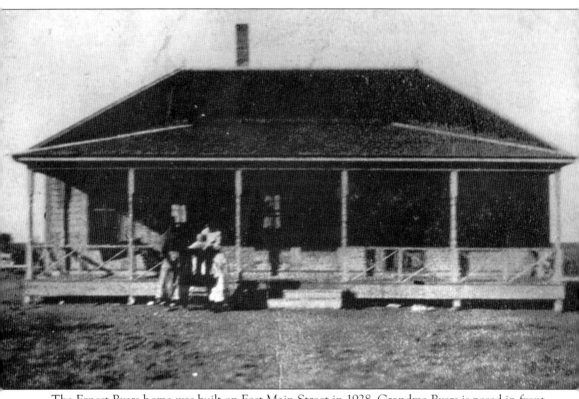
The Ernest Byers home was built on East Main Street in 1928. Grandma Byers is posed in front of her residence in a white dress. (Courtesy Ernest Byers.)

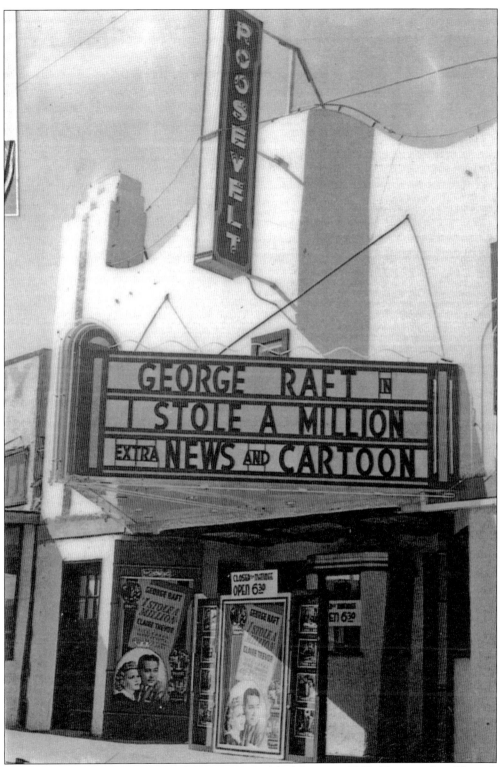
The Roosevelt Theater was located at 120 East Carlsbad Street in 1937. (Courtesy Lois Troutt.)

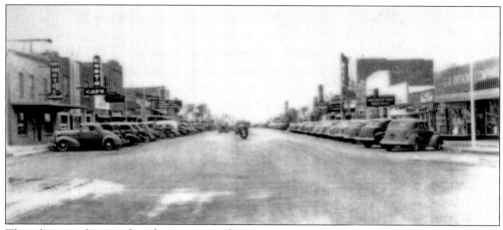
This photograph was taken facing east at the intersection of West Broadway and Linam Street in 1939. (Courtesy Lois Troutt.)

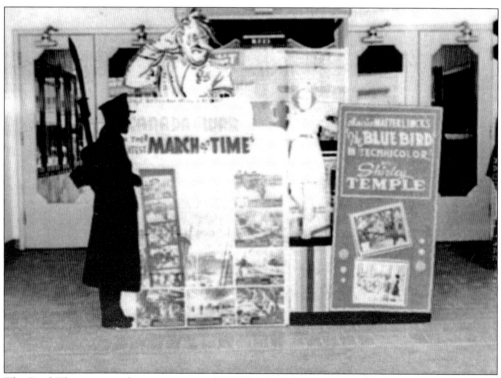
The Reel Theater was playing movies at 209 West Broadway in 1942. (Courtesy Lois Troutt.)

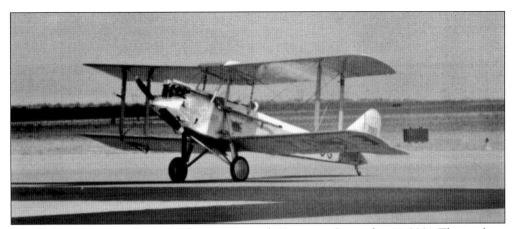

Pilot Carlene Mendieta landed at the Lea Regional Airport on September 11, 2001. The airplane was built in England in 1928. This Avro-Avian is an exact replica of the one flown by Amelia Earhart on a cross-country flight in 1928. Earhart made an emergency landing in Hobbs, spent the night, and continued her flight the next day. She landed on East Broadway. At that time, East Broadway was known as Carlsbad Street and was unpaved. (Courtesy Max Clampitt.)

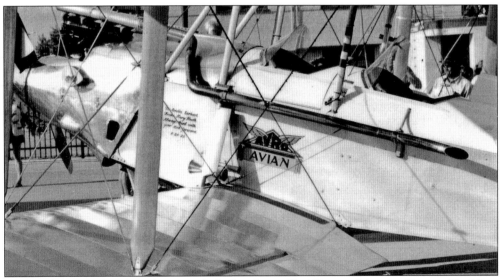

Pilot Carlene Mendieta's airplane was docked in front of Lea Regional Airport Terminal building on September 11, 2001. Mendieta landed in Hobbs on September 10, 2001, for a reenactment flight of Earhart's 1928 cross-country trip. Mendieta was grounded here for several days until airports nationwide were reopened following the 9/11 tragedy. (Courtesy Max Clampitt.)

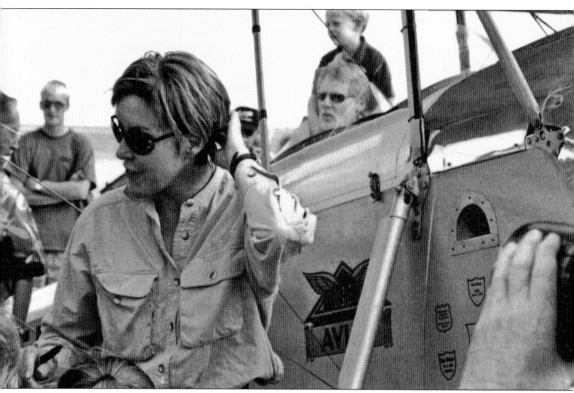

Carlene Mendieta greets the large crowd following her landing at the Lea Regional Airport Terminal building on September 10, 2001. Mendieta is a dentist in Pinole, California. She was required to install a radio and navigation equipment under Federal Aviation Association (FAA) regulations. (Courtesy Max Clampitt.)

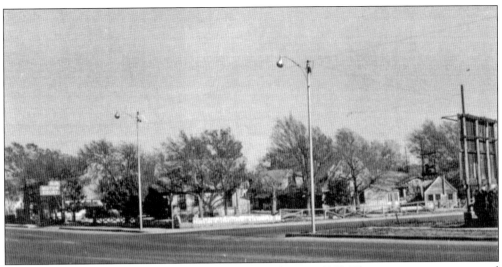

The Barton Motor Court was built at 401 East Broadway in 1975. The motor court was owned by Roy Barton. (Courtesy Naomi Hogue.)

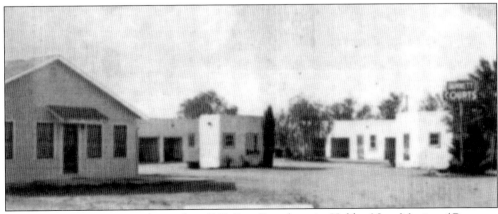

The Bennett's Courts was located at 1223 East Broadway in Hobbs, New Mexico. (Courtesy Naomi Hogue.)

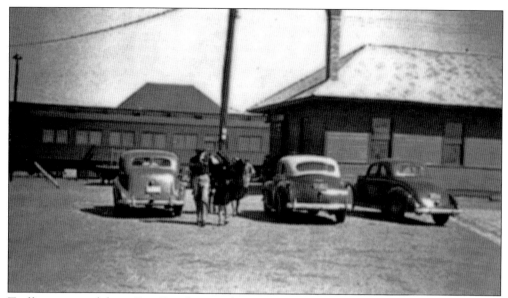

Traffic commuted down East Broadway in the 1930s in Hobbs, New Mexico. The railroad depot was located on the southeast corner in the 600 block of West Dunnam Street in 1943. (Courtesy Naomi Hogue.)

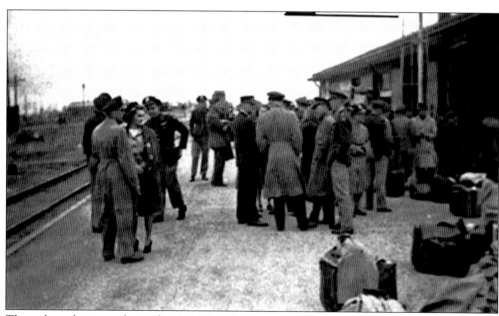

The railway depot was located at 700 West Broadway in 1943. Notice the number of servicemen and their wives. (Courtesy Naomi Hogue.)

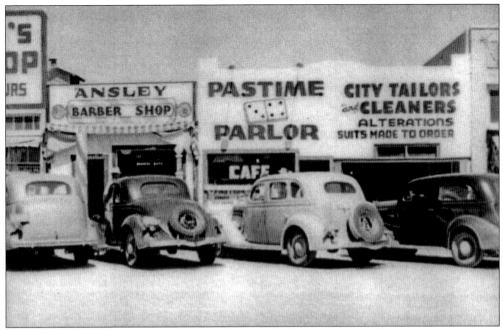

Shops on East Broadway in 1937 included the Ansley barbershop, the Pastime Parlor, and the City Tailors and Cleaners. (Courtesy Johnny Burgess.)

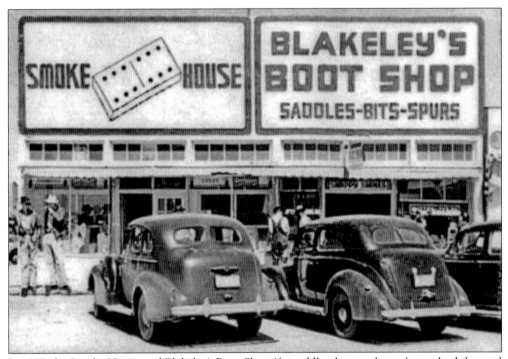

In 1937, the Smoke House and Blakeley's Boot Shop (for saddles, bits, and spurs) were both located on East Broadway. (Courtesy Johnny Burgess.)

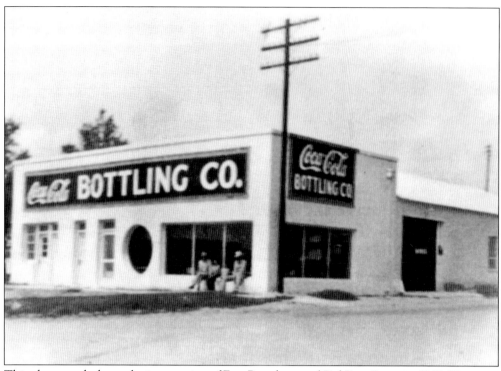

This photograph shows the intersection of East Broadway and Dal Paso Street in 1947. (Courtesy Naomi Hogue.)

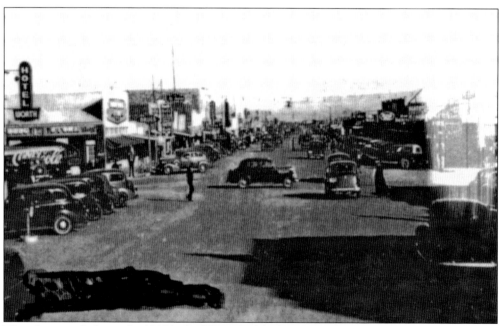

This photograph shows the 100 block of West Carlsbad Street with Shipp Street in the foreground in 1935. (Courtesy Naomi Hogue.)

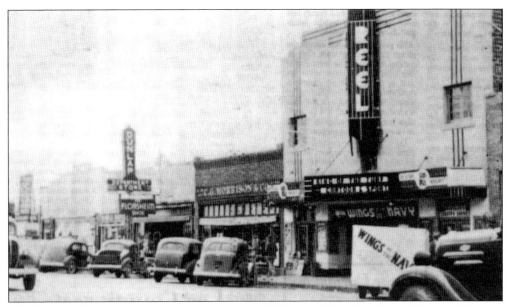
The Dunlaps department store was located in the 200 block of West Broadway. This establishment served Hobbs and Lea County from 1938 to 1990. (Courtesy Joe Harvey.)

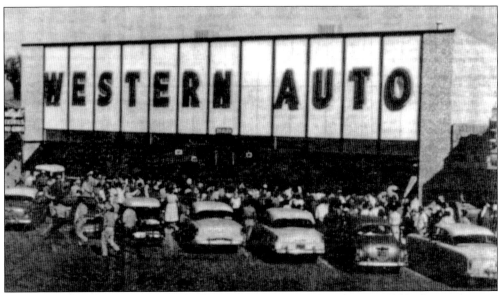
Zearl Young's Western Auto was the hottest attraction on Broadway in 1959 when customers lined up for the grand opening of what would lead to a dynasty of stores. Western Auto's original location was beside the former post office on Taylor Street. (Courtesy Joe Harvey.)

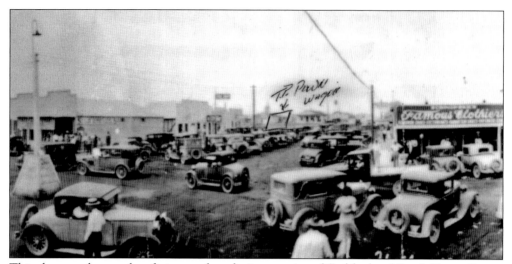
This photograph was taken facing south at the intersection of Carlsbad and South Turner Streets in 1930. (Courtesy Lois Troutt.)

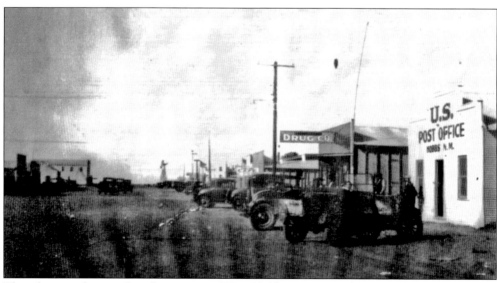
This photograph was taken facing west of New Hobbs in 1929 at the intersection of Main and Dal Paso Streets. (Courtesy Lois Troutt.)

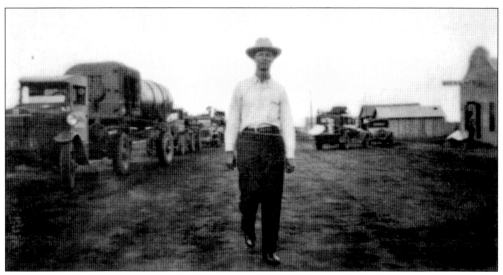

In 1929, B. F. Walker stood next to a tank truck and the City Café on Carlsbad Street. Walker built a large trucking company over the years. (Courtesy Lois Troutt.)

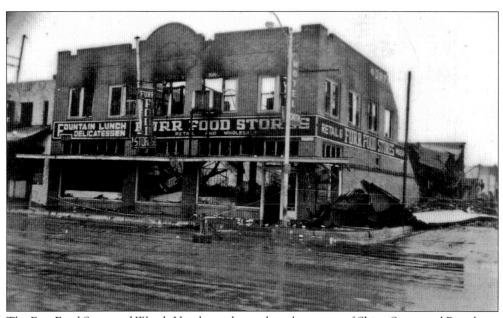

The Furr Food Store and Worth Hotel were located on the corner of Shipp Street and Broadway. Both stores were destroyed by fire in 1939. (Courtesy Lois Troutt.)

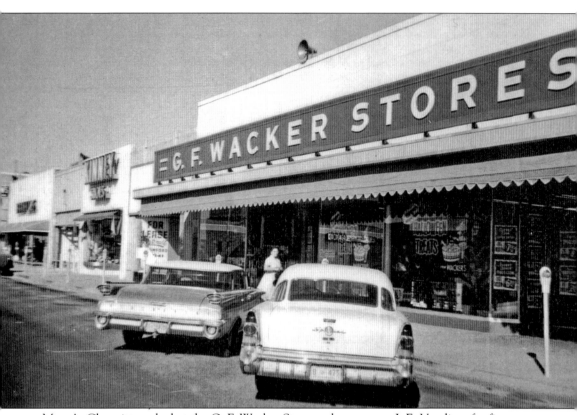

Max A. Clampitt worked at the G. F. Wacker Store under manager J. E. Vandiver for five years in the late 1940s. The store was located at 109 West Broadway. (Courtesy Joe Harvey.)

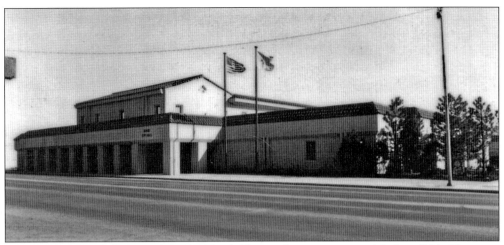
The Hobbs City Hall, located at 300 North Turner Street, was remodeled in 1974. (Courtesy City of Hobbs.)

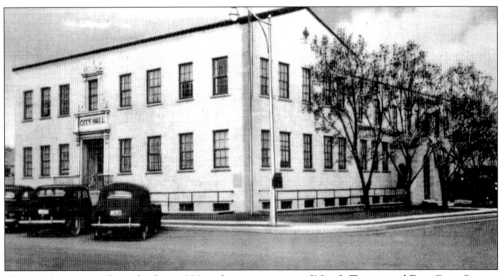
The Hobbs City Hall was built in 1939 at the intersection of North Turner and East Cain Streets and was remodeled again in 1984. (Courtesy City of Hobbs.)

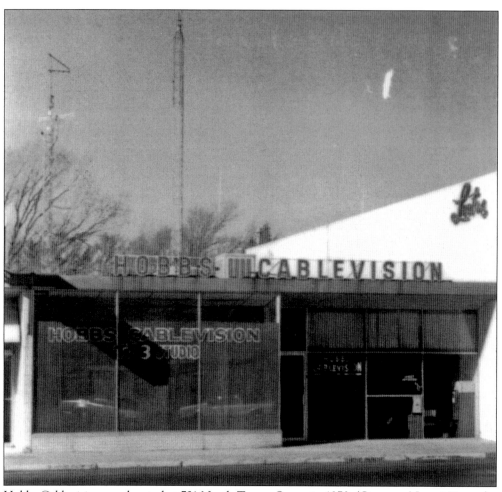

Hobbs Cablevision was located at 721 North Turner Street in 1970. (Courtesy Naomi Hogue.)

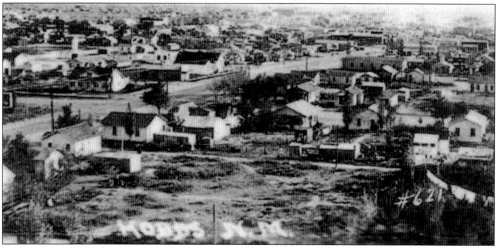

This photograph was taken of the 500 block of North Turner and West Park Streets. (Courtesy Naomi Hogue.)

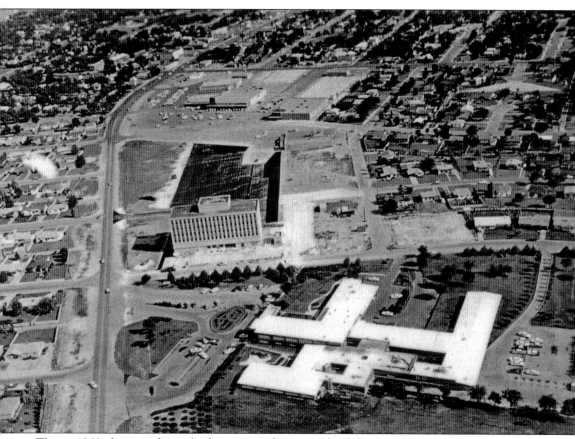
This c. 1960 photograph is a bird's-eye view facing south of the Broadmoor Shopping Center. (Courtesy City of Hobbs, Engineering Department.)

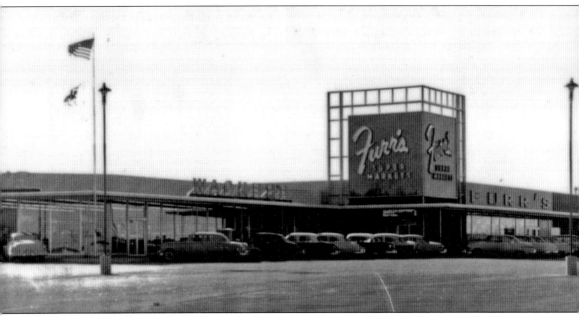

Furr's Supermarket was located near the Broadmoor Shopping Center in the late 1950s. (Courtesy Joe Harvey.)

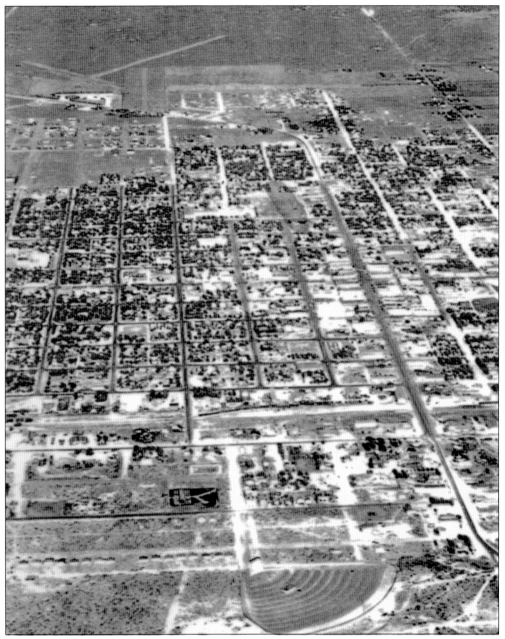
This is a 1950s aerial photograph of Hobbs facing east. The Eagle Drive-in theater was located in the bottom foreground. La Miradora Night Club was near the air strip with the Seminole Highway in front of it. (Courtesy City of Hobbs, Engineering Department.)

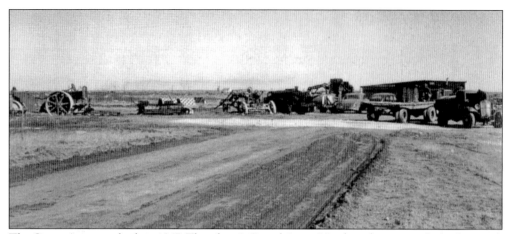

The Green Acres was built in 1947. The white J. C. and Agnes Head residence is in the background, and the two-story windmill can be seen on North Jefferson Street. (Courtesy City of Hobbs, Engineering Department.)

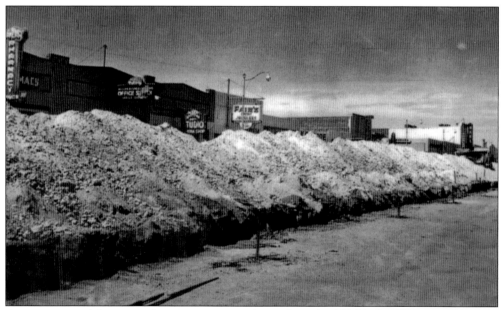

An extension of the storm drainage sewer was located on the 100 block of West Broadway in 1949. (Courtesy City of Hobbs, Engineering Department.)

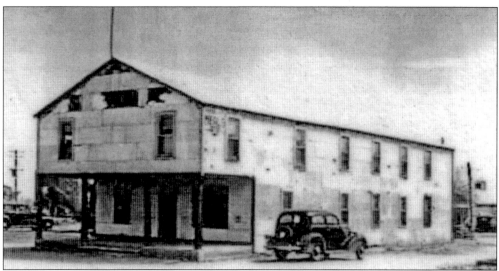

A hotel and café were located in the 400 block of West Broadway in 1935, as shown in this photograph above. (Courtesy Ed Seabourne.)

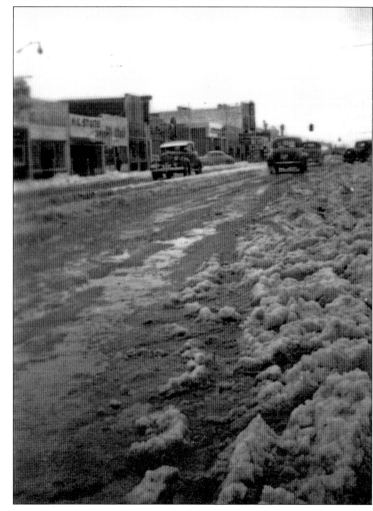

The aftermath of a snowstorm in 1939 is clearly shown from the intersection of Turner Street and West Broadway, facing west. (Courtesy Ed Seabourne.)

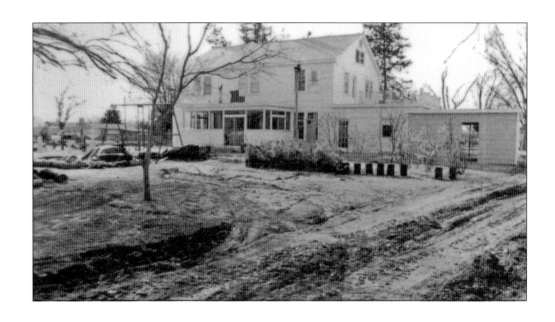

The home of J. C. and Agnes Head, pictured above and below, was located at 1826 North Jefferson Street. J. C. owned a hardware store known as the "Army Store." He was also the mayor of Hobbs in the late 1930s. Agnes published the *Lovington Leader* and *Hobbs Flare* newspapers. (Both, courtesy Naomi Hogue.)

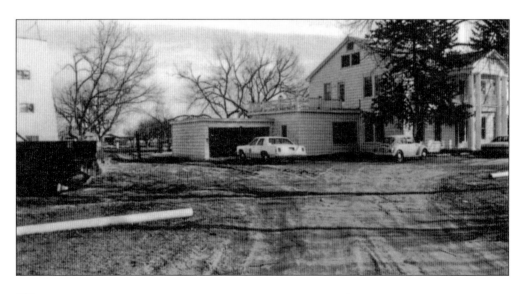

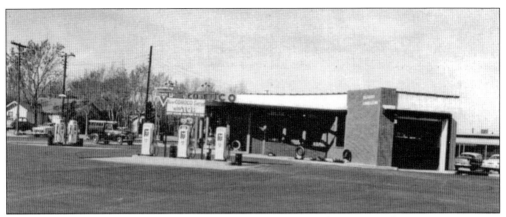
What was the McPeter's Conoco Station on the corner of North Turner and West Sanger Streets is currently a Wendy's hamburger fast-food restaurant. (Courtesy Joe Harvey.)

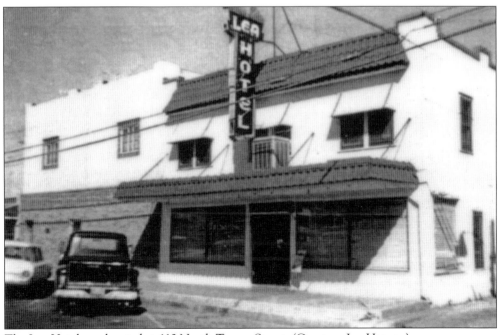
The Lea Hotel was located at 110 North Turner Street. (Courtesy Joe Harvey.)

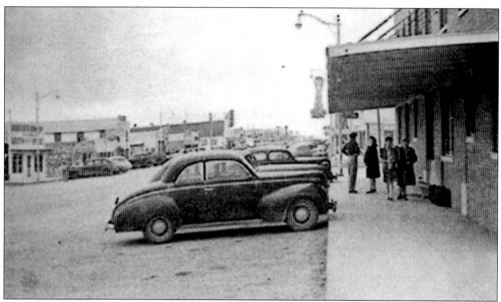

The Frey Hotel was located at 300 East Broadway in 1939. (Courtesy Ed Seabourne.)

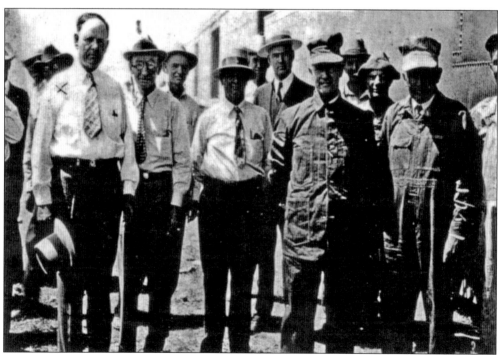

Former governor Dick Dillon is shown standing fourth from the left, dressed in an engineer's cap and overall suit, as he brought the first train to Lea County. The late Wesley McAlester is shown at left holding a straw hat. Next to Governor Dillon is C. L. Yeager (fifth from left), who was the Republican chairman at that time; he now resides in El Paso. Others in the June 28, 1930, photograph could not be identified. (Courtesy Ed Seabourne.)

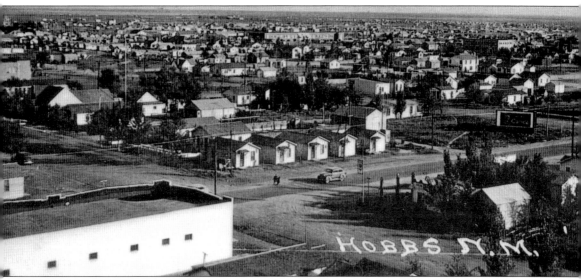

The water tower on North Shipp Street was located near the Masonic Hall, which is in the bottom left of this photograph. Hobbs High School is in the top center, and the Frey Hotel is at the top right. (Courtesy Johnny Burgess.)

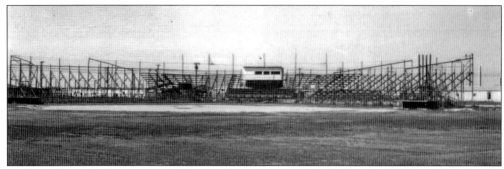

In the 1950s, Bender Park was the home for professional baseball and softball teams in Hobbs, New Mexico. Later, in the 1960s, the high school played their games there, and it was once home to the West Texas–New Mexico League, Sophomore League, and others. (Courtesy Jim Rawls.)

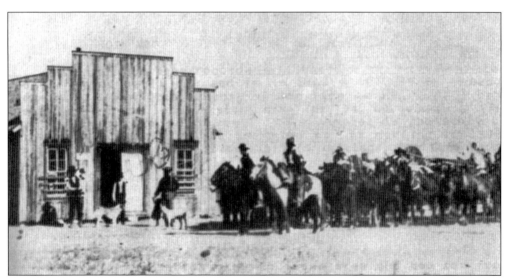

On May 18, 1908, the Hobbs wagon train arrived at the Bronco Store, which was 12 miles from the old Holloway Ranch. The man at the far left is H. Field holding his son Herbert Field in his arms. The elder Field started the Bronco Store. To the right is Kinch Manning, who was postmaster and had the telephone central to which the wire fence phones were connected. Albert Reed is behind him with one of his children. The young men on the lead horses are T. J. "Comy" Reed (left) and Luther Reed (right). Betty Reed Smith is shown in one of the wagons, and "Grandpa" Reed is in the other. (Courtesy Naomi Reed Harris.)

About the Author

Max A. Clampitt is a freelance writer for the *Hobbs News-Sun*. He moved with his parents to Hobbs in 1937 and graduated from Hobbs High School in 1942. He attended New Mexico A&M in Las Cruces for a year and enlisted in the U.S. Marine Corps in August 1943. Clampitt served 27 months in the South Pacific. Discharged in February 1946, he was recalled to active duty for the Korean War, served 17 months, and was discharged with the rank of sergeant in 1953. Clampitt worked at the Hobbs Post Office for 28 years, retiring in 1988. Elected to the Hobbs City Commission in 1972, he served for 20 years as a city commissioner and mayor. He had previously lived in Eunice, New Mexico, for about 15 years, where he served as mayor pro tem and city councilman. He has a large collection of photographs covering Hobbs and Lea County history dating back as far as the 1890s.

Across America, People are Discovering Something Wonderful. *Their Heritage.*

Arcadia Publishing is the leading local history publisher in the United States. With more than 4,000 titles in print and hundreds of new titles released every year, Arcadia has extensive specialized experience chronicling the history of communities and celebrating America's hidden stories, bringing to life the people, places, and events from the past. To discover the history of other communities across the nation, please visit:

www.arcadiapublishing.com

Customized search tools allow you to find regional history books about the town where you grew up, the cities where your friends and family live, the town where your parents met, or even that retirement spot you've been dreaming about.

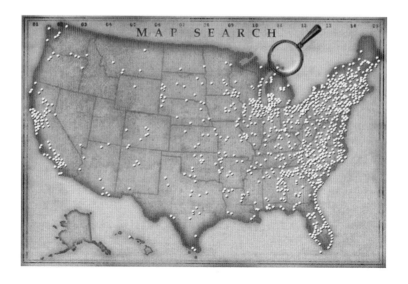